THE HISTORY OF
TORTURE

BRIAN INNES

amber
BOOKS

This new edition published in 2017

Copyright © 2017 Amber Books Ltd

First published in 1998

Published by
Amber Books Ltd
74–77 White Lion Street
London
N1 9PF
United Kingdom
www.amberbooks.co.uk
Appstore: itunes.com/apps/amberbooksltd
Facebook: www.facebook.com/amberbooks
Twitter: @amberbooks

ISBN: 978-1-78274-519-8

Additional text by Martin J. Dougherty
Project Editor: Brian Burns
Picture Research: Adrian Bentley
Design: Colin Hawes

Printed in China

Contents

Introduction

Torture is a vile and depraved invasion of the rights and dignity of an individual, a crime against humanity, for which there can be no possible justification. Or can there? In November 1956, in Algiers, Paul Teitgen faced the ultimate dilemma.

A hero of the French Resistance who had been tortured repeatedly by the Germans in Dachau concentration camp during World War II, Teitgen was now secretary-general at the Algiers prefecture. Fernand Yveton, a communist supporter of the nationalist revolution, had been caught red-handed setting a bomb in the gasworks where he was an employee. But there was a second bomb that was yet to be found; if it exploded many hundreds of lives might be lost. Yveton refused to divulge where it had been hidden, and the Chief of Police tried desperately to persuade Teitgen to let him use all the means of interrogation at his disposal:

> But I refused to have him tortured. I trembled the whole afternoon. Finally the bomb did not go off. Thank God I was right. Because if you once get into the business of torture, you're lost ... Understand, fear is the basis of it all. All our so-called civilization is covered with a veneer. Scratch it, and underneath you find *fear*. The French – even the Germans – are not torturers by nature. But when you see the throats of your *copains* slit, the veneer vanishes.

In an issue of the American magazine *Newsweek* in 1992, Michael Levin, a New York professor of philosophy, considered such a predicament in an article entitled 'The case for torture':

> There are situations in which it is not merely permissible, but morally mandatory, to torture. Suppose a terrorist has hidden a bomb on Manhattan Island, which will detonate at noon on 4 July – unless ... Suppose, further, that he is caught at 10 am that fateful day, but – preferring death to failure – won't disclose where the bomb is ... If the only way to save those lives is to subject the terrorist to the most excruciating possible pain, what grounds can there be for not doing so? I suggest there are none ... Torture only the obviously guilty, and only for the sake of saving innocents, and the line between Us and Them will

(Opposite) The stocks, a common form of punishment in England for five centuries. Titus Oates invented details of a non-existent plot to assassinate King Charles II, which led to the execution of 35 innocent people. In 1685 he was convicted of perjury. He was tied to a cart, and flogged all the way from Aldgate to the pillory at Newgate, and, after two days, flogged from Newgate to Tyburn.

remain clear. There is little danger that the western democracies will lose their way if they choose to inflict pain as one way of preserving order.

At first sight, this argument seems irrefutable. But Amnesty International, the organization dedicated to human rights and above all to the fight against torture, pursued the argument to its logical conclusions:

A man admits to planting a bomb: torture will save lives. A man is suspected of planting a bomb: torture will reveal it. A man has a friend suspected of planting a bomb: torture will lead us to the suspect. A man has dangerous opinions and might be thinking of planting a bomb: torture will reveal his plans. A man knows the one with dangerous opinions and probably thinks the same: torture will lead us to still others. A man has refused to say where a suspect is: torture will intimidate others who might do the same.

The French writer Albert Camus. He was born in Algeria, but later moved to Paris to work as a journalist. During World War II he was active in the French Resistance. Author of several outstanding novels, he received the Nobel Prize for Literature in 1957.

As the French Nobel laureate Albert Camus pointed out: 'torture has perhaps saved some, at the expense of honour, by uncovering 30 bombs, but at the same time it has created 50 new terrorists who, operating in some other way and in another place, would cause the death of even more innocent people'.

The official justification for torture has always been the need to obtain information: from a criminal concerning the extent of his crimes, and the names of his accomplices; from a prisoner taken in war, who may have knowledge of his general's intentions; from a heretic, who can be persuaded to confess his beliefs and implicate others; or from a terrorist whose actions can endanger dozens, maybe hundreds, of innocent lives.

Sadly, the application of torture in such instances, in itself inexcusable, has been overshadowed by the fact that it is regarded also as a punishment – an ambivalence that is reflected in

Professor Levin's proposal to 'torture only the obviously guilty'. The inevitable outcome is that the trade of torturer has attracted only the most sadistic of human beings, and that the use of torture has moved away from any practical need to obtain information, or impose a legal penalty for wrongdoing, to allow the more powerful to enjoy the pleasure of inflicting random pain upon the less fortunate.

But of course we – I, the author, you the reader, all 'right-thinking people' – could never torture another human being. You think so? In 1974, in the Interaction Laboratory at the University of Yale, Stanley Milgram and his team set up a project to experiment with human obedience. They advertised for subjects to take part in 'a study on memory'. In an introductory talk, the applicants were told that 'people learn things correctly whenever they get punished for making a mistake'.

Each volunteer experimenter was introduced to a 'learner', who was strapped into a sort of electric chair with his hand on a metal plate, in an adjacent room of the laboratory. The experimenter was seated in front of an instrument panel: on the panel was a row of switches, each labelled with a voltage from 15 to 450 volts. The last four switches were also marked 'Danger: severe shock'.

Under the control of one of Milgram's team, the volunteers were ordered to switch to a higher voltage each time their learners gave a wrong answer. They were unaware that the switches were dummies, and that the learners were only acting when they screamed and begged for mercy as the 'electric shocks' appeared to become more painful. Although many of the volunteers protested at the apparent effects, they continued to obey the orders of the controller, and 26 out of 40 continued administering 'shocks' up to the maximum voltage.

In some cases, the learner stopped crying out, and even though the volunteer was fearful that he or she was unconscious, or even dead, he still obeyed the controller. A Mr Prozi asked: 'What if he is dead in there? I mean, he told me he can't stand the shock, sir. I don't mean to be rude, but I think you should look in on him.' *I don't mean to be rude!* As Milgram remarked, 'the subject ... thinks he is killing someone and yet he uses the language of the tea table'.

Even more disturbing was the behaviour of a Mr Batta. His 'victim' was seated beside him in the same room and, when the man refused to keep his hand on the metal plate after the 150-volt 'shock', he simply forced it down. Milgram wrote: 'What is extraordinary is his apparent total indifference to the learner: he hardly takes cognizance of him as a human being. Meanwhile he relates to the experimenter in a submissive and courteous fashion.'

'the subject ... thinks he is killing someone and yet he uses the language of the tea table'

Stanley Milgram with the 'electric generator' he used in the Interaction Laboratory at the University of Yale, in an experiment with human obedience. Grimly, he concluded that 'American democratic society cannot be counted on to insulate its citizens from brutality ... at the direction of a malevolent authority'.

What we all hope would be our own reaction was shown by a Dutchman, Mr Rensaaler, who presumably had experience of the German occupation of the Netherlands during World War II. He obeyed the controller, until he reached the 255-volt level. When told he had to continue because he had no choice, he responded indignantly:

Why don't I have a choice? I came here of my own free will. I thought I could help in a research project. But if I have to hurt somebody to do that – I can't continue. I am very sorry. I think I have gone too far already, probably.

Milgram's conclusions are related to his environment and upbringing, but unfortunately they apply equally to all of us:

The kind of character produced in American democratic society cannot be counted on to insulate its citizens from brutality and inhumane treatment at the direction of a malevolent authority. A substantial proportion of people do what they are told to do, irrespective of the content of the act and without limitation of conscience, so long as they perceive that the command comes from a legitimate authority.

An explanation of the psychological mechanism behind such blind obedience was strikingly developed by Hannah Arendt, in her book *Eichmann in Jerusalem: A Report on the Banality of Evil* (1965). In considering how 'ordinary Germans' could face the order to solve 'the Jewish question' under Nazi rule, an order that Heinrich Himmler himself described as 'the most frightening order an organization could ever receive', she wrote:

Hence the problem was how to overcome not so much their conscience as the animal pity by which all normal men are affected in the presence of physical suffering. The trick used by Himmler – who apparently was rather strongly afflicted with these instinctive reactions himself – was very simple and probably very effective; it consisted in turning these instincts around, as it were, in directing them toward the self. So that instead of saying: What horrible things I did to people! the murderers would be able to say: What horrible things I had to watch in the pursuance of my duties, how heavily the task weighed upon my shoulders!

In an important book, *The Body in Pain* (1985), Elaine Scarry has pointed out how torturers distance themselves from their victims by denying their status as a similar human being. They are reduced to symbols, and their pain, and the forms, instruments and places of torture, are given banal names taken from everyday life.

The act of torture may be known as the 'dance' in Argentina, the 'birthday party' in the Philippines, the '*hors d'oeuvres*', 'tea party', or 'tea party with toast' in Greece. The inflicted pain has been called the 'telephone' in Brazil, 'plane ride' in Vietnam, 'motorola' in Greece, and 'the San Juanica Bridge' in the Philippines.

Elaine Scarry sums up this aspect of torture:

> Through the torturer's language, his actions, and the physical setting, the world is brought to the prisoner in three rings: the random technological and cultural embodiments of civilization overarch the two primary social institutions of medicine and law, which in turn overarch the basic unit of shelter, the room. Just as the prisoner's confession makes visible the contraction and closing in of his universe, so the torturer re-enacts this world collapse. Civilization is brought to the prisoner and in his presence annihilated in the very process by which it is being made to annihilate him.

These are modern examples of torture, and it is a sad truth that it is still used, at least semi-legally, in many parts of the world. The present volume is devoted largely to a history of torture, a description of the torment suffered by victims, and the means and specific instruments designed to inflict that torment, through the centuries. But, as Amnesty International repeatedly reveals, the brutality continues, no longer directed only at those regarded as enemies of the state, but at any unfortunate innocent who accidentally attracts the attention of the state's bully-boys.

As the Scots poet Robert Burns wrote, two centuries ago:

Man's inhumanity to man
Makes countless thousands mourn.

'What horrible things I had to watch in the pursuance of my duties'

Chapter One

Torture in Greece & Rome

However repugnant the practice of torture may appear to us today, one very important point must be borne in mind: for at least three thousand years it was legal, and in fact formed a part of most legal codes in Europe and the Far East. There is no mention of torture in the Babylonian or Jewish systems of law, but there is evidence that the Assyrians and Egyptians made use of it: perhaps the earliest recorded reference is the description by an Egyptian poet of how the pharaoh Ramses II, around 1300 BC, tortured some unfortunate prisoners in an attempt to learn the dispositions of enemy forces during the Hittite invasion of Egypt.

At that time, prisoners of war were either slaughtered on the spot, or taken into slavery – and, as slaves, they were regarded as fit for torture. In ancient Greece, too, prisoners were tortured. In his account of the Peloponnesian War (431–404 BC), Thucydides describes how the captured Athenian general Demosthenes was put to death by the Corinthians and Syracusans because they feared that he might be tortured by their Spartan allies, and so reveal their traitorous dealings with the Athenians.

However, in civil law most Greek states did not normally allow the torture of free citizens. On the other hand, slaves and foreigners – none of whom had any legal standing within Greek society – were unprotected. Slaves, in particular, were regarded as suitable substitutes for their owners. In legal proceedings, it was common for the litigants to offer their own slaves for torture, or to request the right to torture those of the opposing party.

The torture was usually carried out in public, and litigants were entitled to perform it themselves. But generally they made use of the civic torturer, the *basanistes* (frequently himself a former slave), because it was considered degrading for free men to indulge in such practices.

There were exceptions to this general rule. In matters of state, particularly cases of treason, the government could demand slaves for torture. And if a citizen was found guilty in such a case, his punishment might well include torture.

(Opposite) The inventor Perilaus designed a brazen bull as an instrument of torture for the Greek tyrant Phalaris. The victim was to be placed inside the bull's belly, and a fire lit beneath it. Phalaris suggested that Perilaus should demonstrate his invention, shut him inside the bull – and ordered the fire to be lit.

Prisoners seized by the Egyptians in warfare were taken into slavery, and could be flogged at will. About 1300 BC, the pharaoh Ramses II tortured prisoners in an attempt to discover the whereabouts of enemy forces during the Hittite invasion of Egypt.

Even the most enlightened philosophers accepted the use of torture. In his conception of the ideal state, Eutopia, Plato admitted the need for double standards: one law for the free man, and another for the slave. A slave could be flogged for an offence that, in the case of a free man, would attract only censure; and, where a citizen might be punished by no more than the imposition of a fine, a slave could be put to death.

The principal legal purpose of torture was to obtain information not given freely. Since citizens could not normally be tortured, evidence had to be obtained from those likely to be privy to their master's affairs. But the value of this evidence was doubtful. As Aristotle declared:

> If it is in our favour, we can exaggerate its importance by asserting that it is the only true kind of evidence; but if it is against us and in favour of our opponents, we can destroy its value by telling the truth about all kinds of torture generally …

A case of murder in Ancient Greece gives us some idea of how much significance was given to testimony of this kind – and it has as much application today. A merchant named Herodes had disappeared on a voyage from Mytilene, and his companion Euxitheus was accused, by one of his slaves under torture, of his murder. The orator Antiphon appeared for the defence, and told the court:

> You have listened to evidence for the length of delay before the man's examination under torture; now notice the actual character of that examination. The slave was doubtless promised his freedom: it was certainly to the prosecution alone that he could look for release from his sufferings. Probably both these considerations induced him to make false charges, which he did. He hoped to gain his freedom, and his one wish was to end the torture. I need not remind you, I think, that witnesses under torture are biased in favour of those who do most of the torturing. They will say anything to gratify them.

We know the sort of tortures that Athenian slaves suffered, from a passage in Aristophanes's *The Frogs* (c. 406 BC). Xanthus, the servant of Bacchus, goes into the underworld pretending to be Hercules, with Bacchus disguised as his slave. Aeacus, one of the judges of hell, challenges the pair, and Xanthus offers his 'slave' for torture:

> *Aeacus* How am I to torture him?
> *Xanthus* In every way: by tying him to a ladder, by suspending him, by scourging him with a whip, by cudgelling him, by racking him, and further, by pouring vinegar into his nostrils, by heaping bricks on him, and every other way …

Tortures of the tyrants

In earlier times, Grecian states had been ruled by 'tyrants' – wealthy men who seized power unconstitutionally. Many centuries later, the Roman writer Valerius Maximus related a number of anecdotes that he had collected concerning the use of torture by these rulers. According to Valerius, the philosopher Zeno of Elea had been involved in a plot to overthrow the tyrant Niarchos, and was tortured to name his accomplices. However, when the pain became too much to bear, Zeno told his tormentors that he would only reveal his secrets to Niarchos in private; and when the tyrant bent down low to hear Zeno's whisper, the philosopher bit off his ear.

Another victim was 'the virtuous Theodore', who suffered flogging, the rack, and branding with red-hot irons, without divulging the names of his fellow conspirators against the tyrant Hieronymos. Finally, he named Hieronymos's right-hand man, whom the tyrant immediately killed, in a fury, before he realized he had been deceived.

when the tyrant bent down low to hear Zeno's whisper, the philosopher bit off his ear

According to the Greek historian Polybius, the tyrant Nabis had an instrument reminiscent of the medieval German *Jungfernkuss* (virgin's kiss), sometimes known as the 'bride of Nuremberg', which was also reputedly used by the Spanish Inquisition (see Chapter 8, pages 135–6):

> This machine, if indeed it may be called by such a name, was an image of a woman, magnificently dressed, and formed in a most exact resemblance of his wife. And when his intention was to draw money from any of the citizens, he invited them to his house, and at first with such civility represented to them the danger with which their country was threatened from the Achaeans; the number of mercenaries which he was forced to retain, etc. But if all his solicitations were without effect, he then used to say: I want, it seems, the power of persuasion; but Agepa, I believe, will be able to persuade you. Agepa was the name of his wife.
>
> Upon these words, the image of the woman that has been mentioned immediately appeared. Nabis then, taking her by the hand, raised her from her seat; and folding afterwards his arms round the person whom he had been soliciting, brought him near by degrees to the body of the image, whose breasts, hands, and arms, were stuck full with points of iron, concealed under her clothes; and then, pressing the back of the pretended woman with his hands, by the means of some secret springs he fixed the man close to her breast, and soon forced him to promise all that he desired.

Under the Roman emperors, torture was regularly employed, particularly if treason was suspected. This 16th-century engraving by Georgio Ghisi is an impression of the conditions of victims in the reign of Julius Caesar.

Another torture machine was the brazen bull designed for the tyrant Phalaris by a man named Perilaus, and described by the second-century satirist Lucian. The bull was lifesize; its interior was hollow, with a trapdoor at the rear for entry. The inventor explained to Phalaris how an offender was to be shut inside the bull's body, while a fire was lit beneath its belly, and, by means of an ingenious arrangement of musical pipes within the bull's head, the victim's screams of pain would be converted into a mellifluous lowing. Lucian related the story as if it were being told by Phalaris himself:

> 'Well now, Perilaus,' I said, 'if you are so sure of your contrivance, give us a proof of it on the spot: mount up and get in and imitate the cries of a man tortured in it, that we may hear whether such charming music will proceed from it, as you make us believe.' Perilaus obeyed, and no sooner was he in the belly of the bull than I shut the aperture, and put fire beneath it. 'Take that,' said I, 'as the only recompense such a piece of art is worth, and chant us the first specimen of the charming notes of which you are the inventor!' And so the barbarous wretch suffered what he had well merited by such an infamous application of his mechanical talent. However, that the noble work should not be contaminated by his dying there, I ordered him drawn out while still alive, and thrown down from the summit of the rock, where his body was left unburied.

The psychopathic monster Caligula, emperor of Rome. He enjoyed inflicting a torture similar to the Chinese 'death of a thousand cuts', so that, as he himself put it, the victim could 'feel himself die'.

Under Roman law also, slaves and foreigners could be tortured. But there was a difference from Greek law: 'A slave who confesses something against his master must not be believed, for it would not do for the lives of masters to be put away at the discretion of their slaves.' This rule applied even in cases where slaves were supposed to be accomplices to their masters' crimes, except in matters of treason, adultery, or incest.

An accusation of one of these crimes – and also a case of a woman accused of poisoning her husband – could bring the accused to the *quaestio*, the judicial inquiry that permitted the use of torture. Under the Roman emperors, and particularly those converted to Christianity, the charge of magic or sorcery was also included.

Treason – or the suspicion of it – invariably brought about the use of torture. In AD 31, the commander of the Praetorian Guard, Lucius

Emperor Nero denied his involvement in the burning of Rome in AD 64. He said that Christians and Jews were responsible, and claimed that he had obtained proof of this by torturing them.

Aelius Sejanus, allegedly murdered Drusus, the only son of the emperor Tiberius, and was suspected of a plot to depose the emperor himself. Sejanus was put to death, but Tiberius was so panic-stricken that he tortured everyone he mistrusted – and, by mistake, he even racked to death a friend who had inopportunely arrived on a social visit.

One torture that was personally devised by Tiberius, according to the Roman historian Suetonius in his *Lives of the Twelve Caesars*, was to order: '... the poor wretches to drink a great quantity of wine, and presently to tie their members with a lute string, that he might rack them at once with the girding of the string, and with the pressure of urine.'

Tiberius's successor, the monstrous Caligula, enjoyed watching prisoners being tortured while he ate. For certain crimes he ordered a treatment not unlike the Chinese 'death of a thousand cuts' (see Chapter 9, pages 149–50): small and repeated stabs with a knife were made so that, in Caligula's words, the victim could 'feel himself die'. Suetonius reports that he had men sawn in two, that the writer of an insulting satire was burned alive in the Roman circus, and: '... the master of his gladiators and wild beasts he caused to be cramped with irons, and beaten for two days together before his eyes, and did not kill him outright till his brain was putrefied, and offended him with the stench.'

Even the relatively gentle Claudius allowed the torture of conspirators and would-be assassins. Tacitus describes the torture of a knight who made the mistake of wearing a sword when he greeted the emperor, and Claudius's adulterous wife Messalina was also tortured.

The use of sorcery and magic was equally regarded as treasonable, since it was believed that it could be used against the emperor. And, because it competed with the official duties of the priests, it was also heretical. Before the adoption of Christianity in Rome, Christians themselves were treated as heretics. At first, they were tortured to force them to deny Christ, and affirm the sovereignty of the emperor. As Tertullian – one of the earliest Christian writers in Rome – put it in his *Apologeticum* (c. AD 193):

> If other criminals plead 'not guilty' you torture them to make them confess. The Christians alone you torture to make them deny ... Yet, if it were something evil, we should deny our guilt – and you would then use torture to force us to confess it ... You assume that we are criminals from the fact that we confess the Name [that of Christ]; and under torture you try to force us to renounce our confession, so that in effect we are forced to deny the crimes that you presume we were guilty of in the first place ...

The emperor Nero claimed that he himself was not responsible for the burning of Rome in AD 64, asserting that Christians and Jews were the culprits, based on information obtained from them by torture. His favourite place of torture was the gardens of his palace. Some victims were sewn into the skins of wolves, and so torn to pieces by savage dogs; others were daubed with pitch and set alight, 'to act as torches in the night'. The free woman Epicharis, who was accused of conspiracy against the emperor, held out for a whole day of torture while refusing to name her accomplices, before hanging herself with her bodice.

The use of torture as a punishment was widespread in Rome: it might be the whole of the penalty, or precede banishment or death. Citizens were allowed to torture their debtors, locking them up in private prisons until the debts were paid. The Christian emperors decreed that

Tiberius was so panic-stricken that he tortured everyone he mistrusted

anyone found guilty of insulting a priest or a bishop in church should be punished. At first, the penalty was the amputation of both feet and hands, but this was later reduced to the amputation of a single hand. Heresy, and other offences committed against the Church, were punished by flogging.

The gladiatorial contests of Imperial Rome were a specialised form of public execution, providing a popular spectacle. The savage animals let loose in the arena – or even another desperate man – were as much instruments of torture as the lash, the executioner's sword, or the cross.

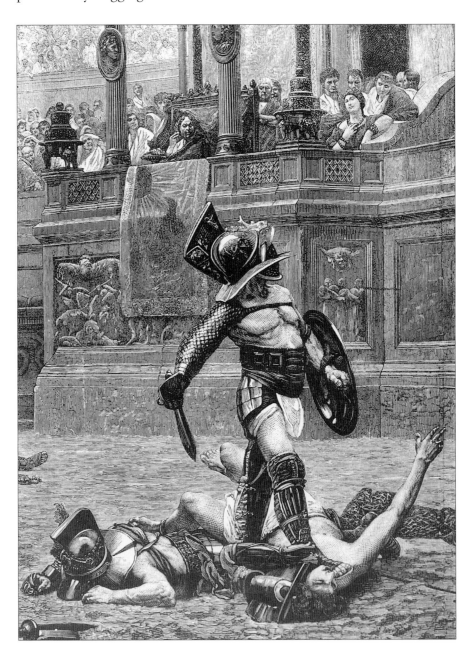

The Roman flogging whip, the *flagellum*, was feared by all. Its thongs, made of ox-leather and sometimes weighted with lead, could cut deep into the flesh. According to Horace, certain judges were so sadistic that they ordered whippings of such length that the executioner was forced to desist, from sheer exhaustion, before the sentence was completed. Many Roman slaves died in the course of their flogging. Lesser penalties were carried out with the *scutica*, a whip with thongs of parchment, or the *ferula*, a flat leather strap.

One of the principal Roman tortures was the *equuleus* – the rack. Its name (Latin for 'young horse') implies that it may have been a frame rather like a vaulting-horse, over which the victim was stretched by weights. Slaves could also be hung by their hands, with weights attached to their feet, and flogged while in this position. Slaves who were sentenced to death were usually crucified, after being arrayed in the *furca* – a V-shaped collar that fitted round the back of the neck and rested on the shoulders – with the hands tied to the thighs, and driven to the place of execution by *carnifices* (literally, butchers) wielding whips.

The lingering torture of death by burning was also practised, particularly by the fourth-century emperor Maximinus, a persistent persecutor of Christians. In his *History of the Martyrs in Palestine* (1861 edition), Eusebius describes the execution of Apphianus:

> The martyr was hung up at a great height, in order that … he might strike terror into all those who were looking on, while at the same time they tore his sides and ribs with combs, till he became one mass of swelling all over, and the appearance of his countenance was completely changed. And for a long time his feet were burning in a sharp fire, so that the flesh of his feet, as it was consumed, dropped like melted wax, and the fire burst into his very bones like dry reeds.

Finally, mention must be made of the gladiatorial contests of Imperial Rome. Few, if any, of the gladiators were willing contestants: they were captives or criminals, merely afforded a different method of execution to entertain the crowds of spectators. The instruments of torture varied – savage lions, bears, tigers, bulls, wolves, mad dogs, or even another equally desperate man – but the outcome was the same. The arena authorities had to exercise strict precautions to ensure that the condemned men did not commit suicide before the performance. But they were not always successful: when the consul Quintus Aurelius Symmachus arranged a display in honour of his son, it was found that the prisoners had strangled one another before the contest.

'at the same time they tore at his sides and ribs with combs, till he became one mass of swelling all over'

Chapter Two
Savage Rituals

When we look at the barbarities practised by ancient cultures such as the Aztecs, or among primitive tribes, it is hard to draw the line between initiatory rites, torture, and ritual sacrifice. For example, the sufferings endured by young men during their rite of passage in the lodge of the Mandan Indians of North America were terrible, and yet they were traditionally undergone by all males, and therefore, to a degree, voluntarily. George Catlin described them in 1841, and in recent years they have been portrayed in the film *A Man Called Horse*:

> The initiate placed himself on his hands and feet. An inch or more of the flesh of each shoulder, or each breast, was taken up between the thumb and finger by a man who held the knife in his right hand, and the knife, which had been ground sharp on both edges, and then hacked and notched with the blade of another to make it produce as much pain as possible, was forced through the flesh below the fingers, and being withdrawn, was followed with a splint or skewer, from the other, who held a bunch of each in his left hand, and was ready to force them through the wound.
>
> There were then two cords lowered from the top of the lodge (by men who were placed on the lodge outside for the purpose), which were fastened to these splints or skewers, and they instantly began to haul him up; he was thus raised until his body was suspended from the ground where he rested, until the knife and a splint were passed through the flesh or integuments in a similar manner on each arm below the shoulder, below the elbow, and below the knees. Each one was then raised with the cords, until the weight of his body was suspended by them, and then while the blood was streaming down their limbs, the bystanders hung upon the splints each man's appropriate shield, bow and quiver, etc.

Catlin noted that the strain upon the flesh at the points where the splints were inserted was so great that it was lifted from the underlying tissues in peaks that were 15 to 20cm (6 to 8ins) high. And in this state the young men hung, desperate to smother their groans and prove their courage and manhood, until the elders of the tribe were satisfied, and allowed them once more to be lowered to the ground, where they lay for a long time almost lifeless.

(Opposite) The North American Indians had practised savage rituals long before white immigrants arrived. In wars between different nations, scalps were frequently taken from defeated foes. Threatened by encroaching settlers, the Indians turned against them, often torturing them in barbaric ways. Robert McGee was scalped by Chief White Turtle in 1864, but survived.

The so-called 'Sun dance' of the Sioux, similar to the initiation ritual of the Mandans. Cords of rawhide are attached to the flesh of the man's breast, and fastened high on a centre pole.

This ritual, even more terrible than the torture of the strappado used in the prisons of the Inquisition (see Chapter 3, page 43), was followed by another ordeal, known as *Eh-ke-nah-ka-nah-pick* (the last race). Each young man had a thick leather strap wound round each wrist, the ends being held by an older warrior on each side of him. Then several heavy weights were attached to his flesh by the same kind of splint as before, and he was dragged, running, round and round in a circle inside the lodge. The movement of the weights generally caused the splints to be gradually ripped from his flesh, and eventually the initiate would collapse from exhaustion and loss of blood.

The avowed purpose of such initiatory rites is, of course, to develop a stoical resistance to pain, which can be of great importance in the harsh conditions of primitive life and in warfare between rival tribes, and to prove that the young man is as strong and brave as his elders. However, one cannot help feeling that at least part of the motivation is the age-old emotion that may be expressed in words such as: 'I had to suffer this as a young man, and you'll just have to learn to put up with it'.

In the light of rituals such as this, it is difficult to decide whether the tortures that native American Indians inflicted upon their captives were solely sadistic, or intended as punishment, or designed to show that the captives were less brave than their captors, and so unworthy of honour. In more modern times, the Japanese in World War II certainly regarded their prisoners with contempt, and treated them accordingly: they believed an honourable man would commit *hara-kiri* sooner than be made prisoner.

The Choctaw (a North American Indian people of Alabama) were reputed to be particularly ingenious in their torture of captives. Their victims were stripped naked, and their arms tied. Then a strong grapevine was looped round their throats, with its other end fastened to the top of a tall pole. In this way a prisoner was free to run around the pole, but remained tethered, like a baited bear. In his *Curiosities of Savage Life* (1863), James Greenwood described what happened next:

> The women make a furious onset with their burning torches; his pain is soon so excruciating that he rushes from the pole with the fury of the most savage beast of prey, lashes them with the trailing vine-rope, and

Indians torturing white settlers with fire. In Texas alone, between 1846 and 1852, some two hundred settlers died under torture by the Apache every year.

bites and kicks and tramples on all he can catch. The circle immediately fills again either with the same or fresh persons; they attack him on every side – now he runs to the pole for shelter, but the flames pursue him ... Should he sink or flag under the torture, they pour over him a quantity of cold water till his spirits recover, and so the like cruelties are renewed until he falls down and happily becomes insensible to pain.

Texas was annexed from Mexico by the United States in 1845, but the Apache knew no frontiers. This Mexican was laid out and tied down, to die slowly in the blistering sun, by the followers of the Apache chief Geronimo.

It has been calculated that in Texas alone between 1846 and 1852 (the years immediately after its annexation from Mexico by the United States), 200 settlers died under torture by the Apache every year. One method was similar to the Chinese 'death by a thousand cuts': victims were tied to a tree, and each day a limb, or a portion of flesh, was cut away. There are also tales of eyes being torn out, and red-hot embers placed in the sockets, or of burning to death over a slow fire. And captured Indians could expect to suffer a similar fate.

After their experiences in the initiatory rites, Indian prisoners were able to bear these pains with legendary stoicism. On the other hand, few white settlers or missionaries were prepared for such suffering, and so

earned their captors' contempt. One who endured his torture with the fortitude of a martyr at the stake was Father Jean de Brébeuf, a member of the Jesuit mission to the Hurons in Canada.

Brébeuf, together with a number of Hurons, was captured by the Iroquois in 1649. First, his hands were chopped off. Then his body was pierced in many places with iron spikes. Tomahawks, heated to redness, were hung around his neck, 'so that every turn of the head was a torment'. A belt of bark, smeared with resin and pitch, was tied around his body and set alight.

The missionary bore his torment bravely. As the torture proceeded, he preached to his captors. Infuriated, they took burning brands from the fire, and stuffed them into his mouth. Even this did not stop his preaching, and eventually the Iroquois cut off his lips.

But Brébeuf was still alive. His captors threw boiling water over him, again and again. The account of his torture reports that they then cut pieces of flesh from his trunk and limbs – carefully avoiding any parts that might be fatal – roasted the flesh, and ate it in front of him. And, before he finally expired, they cut off his feet, and scalped him.

The blood of the Aztecs

Further south, in Mexico itself, prisoners of war were of even greater importance, being necessary for the great blood sacrifices of the Aztecs.

Blood was at the heart of the Aztec religion; it was the source of the Sun's energy. He had to be fed, cooled and kept in motion by the 'red cactus-fruit' – human hearts and blood. If sacrifices were not made regularly, the Sun would stay still in the sky, and the human race would perish from his fire. The most glorious of all warrior deaths was to be sacrificed to the Sun, who kept a special heaven for those who died in this way. But, in this respect, the Aztecs were curiously ambivalent. One of the primary objectives of a warrior was to capture an enemy in battle, and deliver him for sacrifice. So it was generally not the warrior himself but his enemy who was accorded the supreme honour.

This was what happened during the war of 1418–22 between the rival chieftains Netzahualcoyotl and Maxtla. When Maxtla was captured, a special platform was built in Atzcapotzalco for his sacrifice. The warriors surrounded it in their full panoply, their commanders decorated with ornaments of obsidian, jade, and crystal. Maxtla was laid down across a ceremonial block by four attendants, and Netzahualcoyotl himself took the ritual obsidian knife, ripped open Maxtla's breast, and tore out his heart. Maxtla's body was then accorded the full funeral honours of a chieftain.

The most glorious of all warrior deaths was to be sacrificed to the Sun

The Aztec sacrifice to the Sun: prisoners taken in war were led, one by one, up the steps of the Great Pyramid in Tenochtitlán, where their hearts were ripped out with an obsidian knife.

Forty years later, the lands of the Mixtecs to the east were conquered by the Aztecs in a policy of expansion, and the captured warriors were brought back to the Great Pyramid in Tenochtitlán (later Mexico City). One by one they were led up the steps of the pyramid, through clouds of incense. One by one, their hearts were ripped out: a river of blood flowed over the steps, and their bodies were hurled down, to be decapitated and dismembered. The heads were arrayed on a great skull-rack at the top of the pyramid, and the victorious captors were each awarded an arm or thigh. The friar Bernardino de Sahagún, who later wrote a *General History of the Things of New Spain*, reported that these joints were taken home and made into a stew, with chillis and tomatoes, for a ritual meal.

In 1487 the Great Pyramid was rededicated, following another successful Aztec expedition. This saw the greatest of all slaughters. The prisoners were lined up along the causeways into the city of Tenochtitlán, and the blood sacrifices continued for four days. Blood poured down all four sides of the pyramid, which formed huge pools on the pavement below, and literally thousands of skulls were racked up.

Another important deity in the Aztec pantheon was Tlaloc, the spirit of earth, whose ritual site was Mount Tlaloc, the highest point of the sierra. There the annual rainmaking ceremonies were held, with appropriate sacrifices. While these rites were proceeding, another sacrifice was being prepared in the courtyard of the Great Pyramid. A

In Teotihuacan, the huge pyramid dedicated to the Toltec god Quetzalcoatl pre-dates the Aztecs, but this also saw the bloody rites of human sacrifice.

large tree, named Tota, was set up, surrounded by four smaller trees. A young girl – dressed as *Chalchiuhtlicue* ('the jade skirt') – sat within this symbolic forest. When the nobles and priests returned from Mount Tlaloc, the Tota tree was tied to a raft, and rowed out across Lake Tetzcoco, accompanied by the young girl, musicians, and a great crowd of singers in a fleet of canoes. The procession reached the site of a spring at a place called Pantitlán, and the tree was set up beside it. The girl was then sacrificed, and her blood scattered on the water.

The priests who supervised these bloody rites were described by Bernal Díaz del Castillo when the Spanish expedition of Hernán Cortés reached Tenochtitlán in 1519:

> They wore black cloaks like cassocks, and long gowns reaching to their feet. Some had hoods like those worn by canons, and others had smaller hoods like those of Dominicans, and they wore their hair very long, right down to the waist, and some had it even reaching down to the ankles. Their hair was covered with blood, and so matted together that it could not be separated, and their ears were cut to pieces by way of penance. They stank like sulphur, and they had another bad smell like carrion … The nails on their fingers were very long. We heard it said that these priests were very pious, and led good lives.

S BENEDICTVS

INNOCENTIVS EPS SERVVS SERVORV DI. DILECTIS FILII PRIORI ET FRIB IVXTA
SPECV BEATI BENEDICTI REGLARE VITA SERVANTIBVS IN PPTVO. INTER HOLOCAVSTA
VIRTVTV NVLLV MAGIS EST MEDVLLATV QVA ID OFFERTVR ALTISSIMO DE PINGVEDINE
CARITATIS. HOC IGIT ATTENDENTES. CV OLI CAVSA DEVOTIONIS ACCESSISSEM AD LOCV SOLITVDINI
VRE QVE BEATVS BENEDICT SVE CONVERSIONIS PRIMORDIO CONSECRAVIT. ET IVENISSEM VOS IR SECDO
INSTITVTIONE IPIVS LAVDABILITER DNO FAMVLANTES. NE PRO TEPORALIS SVBSTENTATIONIS DEFEC
SPIRITVALIS OBSERVANTIE DISCIPLINA TORPERET. APOSTOLICV VOBIS SVBSIDIV DVXIMVS
IMPENDENDV. SPERANTES ID IDE BEATISSIM BENEDICT NRE DEVOTIONIS AFFECTV SVA RECIB
ET PRECIB APVD PIISSIMV PATRE ET IVSTISSIMV IVDICE COMMDABIT. VRIE ITAQ CVPIETES
NECESSITATIB PVIDERE SEX LIBRAS VSVALIS MONETE VOBIS ET SVCCESSORIB VRIS DE
CAMERA BEATI PETRI SINGVLIS ANNIS PCIPIENDAS CONCESSIM. DONEC INALIVO CERTO LOCO
VOBIS ESSENT VTILITER ASSIGNATE. STATVENTES VT EA QVE ADSVSTENTATIONE VRAM CON
SVEVISTIS PCIPERE DE MONASTERIO SVBLACEN VOBIS ETSVCCESSORIB VRIS PPTER HOC
MINIME NEGARENTVR. POSTMODV AVTE CV REVERSI FVISSEM ADVRBE QVOSDA DE FRIB
VRIS AD NRAM PRESENTIA DESTINASTIS HVMILITER IMPLORANTES VT CONCESSIONE
IPSA INALIVO CERTO LOCO DIGNAREMVR PPETVO STABILIRE. DE AVO PREFATAS
SEX LIBRAS PCIPERE VALERETIS. NOS IGITVR HABITO FRA   RORV CON
ASSENSV. IA DICTAS SEX LIBRAS VOBIS ET SVCCESSORIB VRIS PCIPIENDAS SINGVLIS
ANNIS DE ANNVO CENSV CASTRI PORTIANI CONCEDIM
PRIVILEGIO CONFIRMAN. NVLLI ERGO OMNINO HOMINV LICEAT HANC PAGINA NRE
CONCESSIONIS ET CONSTITVTIONIS INFRINGER VEL
IRE. SIQVIS AVTE HOC ATTEPTARE PRESVPSERIT INDIGNATIONE OMNIPOTETIS DI
ET BEATORV PETRI ET PAVLI APOSTOLORV EIVS SE

Chapter Three

The Inquisition

It is not surprising that the early Christian Church should have spoken out against torture, after its former treatment at the hands of the Roman emperors. At one point, it was even declared a sin for Christians to exercise judicial powers, since the law might require them to use torture in the course of their duties. In 866, Pope Nicholas I clearly expressed the Church's attitude to torture, in a letter to Prince Boris of Bulgaria:

> A confession must be spontaneous, not extracted by force. Will you not be ashamed if no proof emerges from the torture? Do you not recognize how iniquitous your procedure is? If the victim who has not the strength to resist confesses himself guilty, without being so, who is then the criminal – if not the one who has forced him to make a lying confession?

One reason for the Christian opposition to torture was that Greek and Roman law had allowed for the practice to be used principally against slaves, and, since within the Christian world it was not permissible for a Christian to be enslaved by fellow Christians, there was a considerable shortage of available victims.

Legal trials took the form of accuser and accused being heard by a (supposedly) impartial judge, whose duty was to act as arbiter. Both took an oath to affirm that they were telling the truth – and perjury was regarded as a sin that would be instantly punished by God. Both could call into court a number of friends or relatives who also swore, not to any knowledge they might have of the facts of the case, but only to their belief in the solemnity of the oath.

However, the criminal-minded soon discovered that perjury – though it might result in all sorts of torments in the next world – seldom called down the immediate wrath of the Almighty in the present one. The ease with which perjury could lead to a miscarriage of justice led to the development of an alternative process. This was trial by ordeal, which was based upon the belief that 'right conferred might'. There were two sorts of ordeal: those in which both parties took part, and those to which only the accused was submitted.

The first type might be relatively mild, such as requiring the contenders to stand before the crucifix with arms raised, while masses were said: the victor – and therefore the one judged to be in the right

(Opposite) Pope Innocent III issued a Bull banning trial by ordeal in 1215. The result was the establishment, by the Lateran council, of the Holy Inquisition.

– was the one who could keep this up the longer. Or it might take the more violent form of a judicial duel. The two contenders met one another in single combat, in which, again, the victor was adjudged to be the one who had told the truth.

In the second type of ordeal, it was solely the guilt or otherwise of the accused that was to be determined. A piece of consecrated bread might be placed in the accused's mouth – if it could not be swallowed, he was deemed guilty. Alternatively, he could be required to take an oath on a sacred relic. However, there were more severe ordeals, such as submitting limbs – hands, arms, feet, and legs – to red-hot iron or boiling water in the belief that, if the accused was innocent, God would protect them from injury.

In this way, the basic concept of torture gradually crept back into the judicial process. There is plenty of evidence that the threat of the ordeal could induce a suspect to confess; from that it was an easy step to apply the ordeal in order to obtain a confession. The twelfth-century laws of Brittany, for example, stated that in the trial of a suspected murderer:

> If he deny the deed, and be taken red-handed or in pursuit, or the deed be notorious among the people of the parish, it is proper that he submit to inquiry and the proof by witnesses ... and if it cannot be completely proved, and common report or strong presumptions are found against him, he should have ordeal, or torture, three times. And if he can endure the torture or the ordeal without confessing, he shall have saved himself ... and he should go unscathed concerning the deed, and it should be adjudged that he be acquitted and released.

During the twelfth century, trial by ordeal came increasingly under attack, both from lawyers and theologians. The most outspoken was the churchman known as Peter the Chanter, who drew attention to the fact that the requirement to survive the single ordeal without injury was tantamount to seeking a miracle, and so violated the biblical injunction 'thou shalt not tempt the Lord thy God'. He cited numerous cases in which clearly innocent people had failed the ordeal, and had therefore been condemned.

Nevertheless, the ordeal continued for some time. In 1157, the hot iron was ordained by the council of Rheims for everyone suspected of heresy. In 1210, 13 years after Peter the Chanter's death, bishop Henry of Strasbourg ordered the treatment for some 100 heretics. But this time the pope, Innocent III, upheld the appeal of one of the condemned, and in 1215 he banned trial by ordeal.

it was an easy step to apply the ordeal in order to obtain a confession

Trial by ordeal was practised for many centuries before its abolition by the Lateran council in 1215. It was based upon the belief that 'right conferred might', and, in its more extreme form, was intended to reveal the guilt or otherwise of the accused. If he could submit to the red-hot iron, and be innocent, God would protect him from injury.

At the same time, other developments had been taking place, both in ecclesiastical and in secular law. There was a great deal of corruption among the clergy and in the monasteries, and in an effort to root it out clerical judges were given the power to initiate trials on the basis of a denunciation, without requiring the accuser to appear in person, so that they became both judge and prosecutor. Soon, charges of heresy brought against clerics were to be heard in the same way.

The secular courts, meanwhile, had developed a judicial system – *per inquisitionem* (from the Latin meaning 'inquiry') – that had been instituted in the ninth century by the emperor Charlemagne. Bearing the emperor's authority, royal commissioners travelled through his domains, enquiring into, and pronouncing sentence on, matters of dispute, injustice, and crime. When the fourth Lateran council banned trial by ordeal in 1215, it introduced, in its place, the *inquisitio*.

the pattern was set for a new form of religious trial, the Inquisition

So the pattern was set for a new form of religious trial, the Inquisition – initially charged only with the suppression of heresy, although it later concerned itself with other matters – that was to earn itself a sinister reputation in the centuries to come. The Lateran council decreed that any rulers who failed to root out heresy in their kingdoms could be deposed, which led, inevitably, to agreement by the civil authorities that death was the only acceptable penalty for proven heresy. This had occurred as early as 1197 in the Spanish kingdom of Aragon; Lombardy followed suit in 1224, France in 1229, Rome in 1230, Sicily and Naples in 1231, and Germany in 1232. The trigger for this obsession with heresy was the Albigensian Crusade.

The Cathars and the Albigensian Crusade

For centuries, the Roman Church had struggled to eliminate beliefs to which it gave the general name of 'Manicheism'. These derived from a philosophy put forward in the third century by a Persian prince named Mani; aspects of them became absorbed into early Christianity, and even St Augustine had been attracted to them, but the sect that adhered to them was suppressed around AD 600. Nevertheless, a religion that had developed from these beliefs continued to flourish on the fringes of the late Roman Empire, particularly in Bulgaria.

This religion was dualist: put very briefly, it taught that there were two Gods. The 'good' God was very far away, little concerned with the doings of humankind, and certainly not responsible for the occurrence of evil in the cosmos. The other God – the God of the Jews and Christians – was the creator of the physical world and, since that included everything bad, he must himself be disposed to evil. Even human life, the gift of this God, was worthless. It followed that the truly religious should not attempt to prolong life, but should seek death by refusing all meat and drink. Certainly they should not create new life by sexual activity (in recognition of their attempts at sexual abstinence, the name of the Bulgars became *bougres* in French, and 'buggers' in English).

Despite the harsh nature of these basic beliefs, the pure austerity of this religion, at a time when the Roman Catholic Church was under criticism for its ostentation and the dissolute lives of its clergy, proved attractive to many people. With its emphasis on piety, chastity, and poverty, it was seen as being closer to the ideals of early Christianity. Travelling preachers brought the new beliefs westward through northern Italy and into southern France during the early twelfth century; they were known as Cathars, a name probably derived from the Greek, meaning 'pure'.

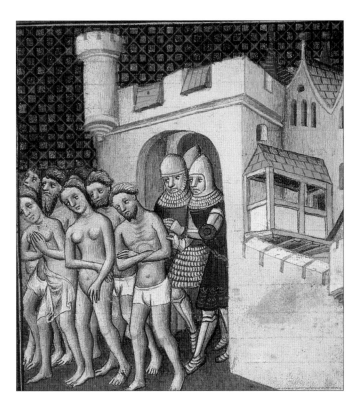

During the Albigensian Crusade, the Cathars, as confirmed heretics, were treated with great brutality. This illustration of their expulsion from the city of Carcassonne comes from The Chronicles of France, *1388.*

Rather than giving up all nourishment, these men (and some women), who were called 'perfects', had taken a solemn vow to renounce the world and all its works, dedicating themselves to God and the gospel, and swearing never to lie or bear false witness, never to have sex, and to eat only vegetables and fish. Their followers, the believers, were permitted a modest relaxation of these rules, and usually took the final vow, the *consolamentum*, only on their deathbeds – an equivalent of the Catholic last rites.

During the twelfth century, the Languedoc, a vast region of south-west France, was not strictly part of the French kingdom: it was a loose confederation nominally under the rule of the counts of Toulouse, who frequently changed their allegiance between France, the English throne, which owned Aquitaine to the west, and the Spanish kingdom of Aragon. It was an area with its own highly developed culture, and its own language, Occitan. Poetry and music were highly valued, particularly the songs and ballads of the native troubadours, and the relaxed climate was one in which Cathar beliefs were deemed acceptable. Here the

Cathars were also known as Albigensians, after the cathedral town of Albi, north-east of Toulouse.

For more than 50 years the Roman Catholic Church tolerated Catharism, which spread rapidly. However, by the turn of the century the Church considered itself threatened by these essentially heretical beliefs. In 1204 the Spanish monk Domingo de Guzmán – founder of the Dominican order in 1216, and the future St Dominic – visited Toulouse, but is said to have converted only a single heretic. In 1207 Pope Innocent III sent two legates to the count of Toulouse, Raymond VI, to request his assistance in suppressing the heresy and converting the Cathars once more to Catholicism. Raymond refused and was excommunicated, and the legates set out to return to Rome; but when they reached the confines of the Languedoc, at the crossing of the Rhône, they were overtaken by armed horsemen, and murdered.

Outraged, the pope declared a crusade against the Albigensians. He attempted to obtain the support of the king of France, Philippe Auguste, but he was occupied in winning back parts of France from England, and was unable, or unwilling, to support the crusade. However, the pope found a suitable champion in Simon de Montfort, Earl of Leicester, who

Simon de Montfort, Earl of Leicester, who had just returned from the Fourth Crusade to the Holy Land, led the Albigensian Crusade for ten years. But, in the siege of Toulouse in 1218, he was killed by a stone catapulted from the city walls.

had just returned from the Fourth Crusade, and who gathered together a group of barons from northern France.

The army that marched south was a motley of battle-hardened veterans, mercenaries, and ragged opportunists. They were required to 'bear the cross' – in red on their tunics – for only six months, after which all their sins would be forgiven; so their numbers and organization constantly changed. But they were more experienced than their opponents, as the inhabitants of the south soon discovered.

The first city of any size that the crusaders encountered in their advance toward Toulouse was Béziers. While Raymond vacillated, unable to make up his mind whether to resist or give in to the pope's demands, the viscount of Béziers had realized that the crusade was really an excuse for the northern barons, and eventually the French king, to take possession of the Languedoc. Most of his subjects, Cathars and Catholics alike, supported him, and when the crusaders, besieging Béziers in 1209, offered to raise the siege in exchange for 222 named heretics, the citizens refused. The army attacked, and the walls were breached. Hundreds crowded into the cathedral for sanctuary, but the crusaders set it on fire. When somebody pointed out to the Abbot of Clairvaux, one of the papal legates with the army, that many of those trapped in the flames were Catholics, he replied: 'Let them all die! God will recognize his own.'

After this holocaust, resistance collapsed for a time: Carcassonne surrendered, and other cities were soon captured. Everywhere, Cathars and others were consigned to the flames: at Lavaur, 400 were burned in a single day. When the castle of Cabaret fell in 1211, the chatelaine was thrown alive into a pit, and covered with stones. Rome decreed that Raymond was to be stripped of his lands, which were awarded to Simon de Montfort and his principal henchmen. But when de Montfort arrived to besiege Toulouse, he was killed by a stone catapulted from the city walls.

The war dragged on intermittently for many years. A number of Cathars took refuge in the mountain fortress of Montségur. They were besieged there in 1243, and in March of the following year, with their water supply polluted and undrinkable, they surrendered. But 205 of them, both men and women, refused to deny their beliefs, and walked singing into the flames of their funeral pyre. Montségur was claimed in the name of King Louis IX, and the Languedoc became part of the lands of France. Eleven years later the last Cathar stronghold, Quéribus, fell.

Meanwhile, Raymond's son, Raymond VII, had appealed for the return of his territories, and promised to wipe out heresy. He welcomed the Dominicans and Franciscans, and in 1229 the Inquisition was set

205 men and women walked singing into the flames of their funeral pyre

When the Cathar
stronghold of Montségur
surrendered in 1244, 205
men and women, secure
in their beliefs, walked
singing into the flames
of their funeral pyre.
But this was not the end
of the persecution of
the Cathars. The castle
of Quéribus held out
until 1255, and the last
Cathar to be burned was
Bélibaste, in 1321.

up in Toulouse, and a violent persecution of heretics began. However, among the peasant population it took nearly a century for Catharist beliefs to be suppressed. The last Cathar to be burned, by the name of Bélibaste, was executed outside the walls of the little castle of Villerouge-Termenés in 1321.

The Inquisition gathers strength

In the beginning, it was intended that the trials of the Inquisition should be supervised by local bishops, but it soon became apparent that they had insufficient knowledge of Canon Law, and their authority extended over too limited a region for them to deal adequately with questions of heresy. In 1231 Gregory IX announced that the arrests and trials of heretics would become the responsibility of the papal Inquisition, controlled from Rome. Two years later, he wrote to the bishops of France:

> We have decided that it is only right to give part of your burden to others, and accordingly to send to the kingdom of France and neighbouring provinces, against the heretics, some Dominican friars. We enjoin that you receive them kindly, and treat them with honour, by giving them such good advice, aid, and support in this office, and in other respects, that they may be able to carry out the task entrusted to them.

The travelling inquisitors were commonly members of the Dominican order, but some were Franciscans, or even members of other orders. Their duties were firstly to seek – 'inquire' – for heresy, making use of local gossip and denunciation. Any suspect was to be summoned to appear before them, and given time to confess and absolve himself; only when this failed was the accused to be prosecuted before the inquisitorial court, interrogated, and tried, with the evidence of any witnesses who were prepared to testify.

The inquisitors were chosen for their learning and piety, and their contemporaries were generally of the opinion that they carried out their duties with a degree of mercy – indeed, some were later canonized as saints. One, St Peter Martyr, has been called 'the patron saint of the Inquisition'. An influential preacher in Lombardy, he was appointed by Gregory IX in 1234 to be chief inquisitor for northern Italy. Although he rigorously punished heretics, the purpose of his mission was to convert them if possible; however, he earned the enmity of many, and was assassinated in 1252. It may well have been the murder of Peter

The travelling inquisitors were commonly members of the Dominican order

St Peter Martyr was appointed chief inquisitor for northern Italy in 1234. He pursued heretics rigorously, but was reputed to be just in his interrogations. He was assassinated in 1252.

that induced Pope Innocent IV to authorize the use of torture by the Inquisition in the same year.

The Inquisition exercised its powers chiefly in Italy, France, the German states, and (for a time) northern Spain – the Spanish Inquisition (see Chapter 5), and the later Roman Inquisition, were separate organizations. In the beginning, trials were held in the local monastery of the order to which the inquisitor belonged. The inquisitors had great authority, and could appoint their own assistants and lawyers. However, the assistance of the civil powers was necessary when it came to imposing the death penalty – and, later, when torture was used – and the kings and princes soon realized that the Church's decree, which made them personally responsible for stamping out heresy, placed immense power in their hands. Declaring themselves 'defenders of the faith', they instituted harsh secular laws over which the Church had no control. Soon, torture was allowed in the investigation of a range of crimes that were not of a religious nature. Particularly in Germany, torture was widely used to induce confessions of guilt, a process that has been described by a modern German historian:

Examination conducted in the torture chamber by personnel of the municipal council; questioning of the accused about all the details; repetition of examination following the intervening arrest of accomplices; extraction of confessions with torture, in case the accused was not prepared, without the application of force, to admit the facts that it was desired to hear from him.

Rules concerning the use of torture by the Inquisition were gradually developed, and codified subsequently by Nicolas Eymeric, papal inquisitor in Aragon during the latter half of the fourteenth century. In his *Directorium Inquisitorum* he wrote:

> One must not resort to the question until other means of discovering the truth have been exhausted. Good manners, subtlety, the exhortations of well-intentioned persons, even frequent meditation and the discomforts of prison, are often sufficient to induce the guilty to confess.

Torture could be used: firstly, in the case of persons who varied in their answers during the course of interrogation; secondly, when the accused had a reputation for heresy, even when no witnesses could be found to testify against them, or where there were several indications or proofs of heretical beliefs; and lastly, even if the accused was not a notorious heretic, but if there was at least one witness, and one or more powerful indications of heresy.

These, at least, were the rules promulgated by Eymeric and reprinted many times in the following century, but there is ample evidence that few papal inquisitors, and certainly no civil authorities, adhered to them.

The accused were condemned to the torture with a formula pronounced by the judge:

> We, by the Grace of God Inquisitor of [name of the administrative region in which the court was held], having carefully considered the proceedings against you, and seeing that you vacillate in your replies and that there are nevertheless many indications against you, sufficient to expose you to the question and torment; in order that the truth may be had from your mouth and that you should cease to offend the ears of the judges, declare, judge and sentence you by an interlocutory order, [at such-and-such a time and day], to undergo torment and torture ...

Prisoners were taken to the torture chamber and stripped by the executioners

Prisoners were then taken to the torture chamber and were stripped by the executioners. They were urged to confess, and might be promised their lives; however, if they had previously abjured their heresy and had relapsed, they would inevitably be 'relaxed' to the secular authorities for burning. In the absence of confession, prisoners would then be tortured – first with the milder methods, while being interrogated on the less serious crimes of which they were accused. They were then shown the worst instruments, and told they must suffer them all until they confessed everything.

Eymeric gives no details of the methods of torture employed by the Inquisition, and they varied from country to country according to the

The strappado, which was widely employed by the Inquisition in Italy, underwent many local variations. In this woodcut from the 16th-century Praxis Criminis Persequendi *('The Technique of Interrogating Criminals'), the victim is suffering not only the strappado, but has a rope gradually twisted tighter about his wrists.*

secular law. In Italy, the most usual method was the strappado, by which victims had their arms tied behind them with rope and were then suspended from a pulley attached to a beam. Writing in 1584, the Florentine lawyer Paulus Grillandus enumerated five degrees of torture, which increased in severity according to the crime.

In the first degree the victim was merely stripped and tied, and threatened with the strappado. Since this involved no real physical pain, it could be done, even without any of the indications necessary for torture, and Grillandus reported that his own experience showed that it was very successful in obtaining confessions from 'weak and timorous persons'. In the second degree, the culprit was raised on the pulley for a brief period – the time taken to recite an Ave Maria, a Paternoster, or a Miserere – but without any shaking or pulling of the rope.

In the third degree, the victim was hung for a longer period, but still without jerking. This was reserved for the fourth degree, and caused excruciating pain. In the fifth degree, weights were attached to the culprit's feet to increase the agony of the jerking rope: the torture usually fractured the bones, and frequently tore limbs from the victim's trunk.

A German document of a later date lays down the regulations for torturing a victim with ropes about the arms:

In the fifth degree, weights were attached to the feet to increase the agony

(i) There must be no jerks, but a gradual tightening and release of the ropes; blows with the ropes, first on one arm and then the other, are permitted.

(ii) Each turn of the rope must be three fingers more than the previous one, for each arm in turn.

(iii) The rope must be tied round the two arms together.

(iv) The knot must not pass above the elbow, and the pull must be applied in such a way as to prevent the knots from loosening.

(v) Penetration of the rope to the bone must not be achieved by jerks, but by a sliding movement of the rope.

(vi) Since blows frequently break the skin, it is a good idea to use this method, which increases the pain according to how hard one strikes the rope.

(vii) When the rope is released on one side, the tension must be maintained on the other.

However, few torturers observed the sadistic nicety of the rules. Hippolytus de Marsiliis, another sixteenth-century lawyer, described some of the (strictly) illegal methods used. A mixture of quicklime and water might be put into the victim's nostrils. As in India (see Chapter 9, page 155), a scratching or biting insect might be caged on a delicate part of the anatomy; or the victim might be bound to a table covered with spiny hawthorn branches. A torture identical with the Chinese *tean zu* (see Chapter 9, page 147) was to place small pieces of wood between the fingers and bind them tightly together. And a variation upon the Chinese bastinado was the notorious 'torture of the goat's tongue', where the victim's feet were covered in salt, and a goat was allowed to lick them. The rough rasping on the soles of the feet resulted in the most exquisite agony, without any physical damage.

It was Hippolytus himself who is credited with one of the most effective forms of torture, and one that caused no physical injury: sleeplessness. The victim was kept awake by a rota of guards, and was shaken or pricked at intervals, or made to walk up and down, for the length of two days and nights, or even more. Combined with a starvation diet, or even complete deprivation of food and water, and the dismal conditions of the prison cell, this soon produced a state of disorientation, in which the victim could be persuaded to say whatever was required. In England, where torture was prohibited under Common Law – in principle! – this became a favoured method in the interrogation of those suspected of witchcraft (see Chapter 7, page 117). In modern times, many regimes have adopted it (see Chapter 12, pages 176–7).

> *One particularly sadistic variation was piercing the nostrils with a thread soaked in pitch*

One particularly sadistic variation was described later by the French lawyer Jean de Grèves: the nostrils were pierced with a thread soaked in pitch, which was tugged at intervals to keep the victim awake. An Italian lawyer described it as the most effective of all tortures: 'out of 100 martyrs exposed to it, not two could endure it without becoming confessors'.

The Templars

The Knights Templar – or Poor Knights of Christ and of the Temple of Solomon – was a military order of monks founded in 1119, by the French crusader Hugues de Payns, to protect pilgrims to Jerusalem from attacks by the Saracens. They obtained the support of Bernard of Clairvaux (later St Bernard), and in 1139 were given important privileges by Pope Innocent II. These included the right to maintain their own chapels, and exemption from the jurisdiction of any bishop.

Although at first the Templars had no castles of their own, their numbers grew rapidly, and soon they were receiving grants of fortresses and lands from many different rulers. They became very powerful, so much so that their Grand Master came to consider himself the equal of any king. They took up banking, lending money (even to the kings of France), and using their 'commanderies' as safe deposits for royal valuables. By the mid-thirteenth century there were Templar establishments all over Europe.

Despite their reputation for chivalry, honesty, and celibacy, there were soon persistent rumours about the Templars' beliefs. As early as 1207, Pope Innocent III had accused them of 'apostatizing from God, scandalizing the Church, and employing doctrines worthy of demons'. In 1304, a certain Esquiu de Floyran reportedly revealed 'the secrets of the Templars' to James II of Aragon, and subsequently took his tale to Philippe IV of France. Philippe suggested to the pope in Avignon, Clement V, that the allegations should be investigated, and in August 1307 the Templars' Grand Master, Jacques de Molay, agreed; at the same time Philippe introduced his own spies into the order.

The following month, after receiving his spies' first reports, Philippe signed an order for the arrest of all Templars in his dominions:

> On the report of persons worthy of trust, We have been informed that the brothers of the military order of the Temple, hiding under the habit of the order as wolves in sheep's clothing, insulting miserably the religion of Our faith, have once more crucified in Our time Our Lord Jesus Christ, already once crucified for the redemption of mankind, and inflicted on Him worse injuries than

Pope Innocent IV authorized the use of torture by the Inquisition in 1252.

He suffered on the cross; when, on entering their order, they make their vows and are presented with His Image and by a sorrow – what shall I say, a miserable blindness – they deny Him thrice and, by a horrible cruelty, spit thrice on His face; after which, divested of the clothes they wore in secular life, they are taken naked into the presence of him whose task it is to receive them and there they are kissed by him … first at the base of the spine, secondly on the navel, and finally on the mouth. And after they have offended against the Divine Law by equally abominable and detestable acts they oblige themselves, by an oath and fearless of the offence against human law, to deliver themselves one to another without refusal – and from this time they are required by this vice to enter into an horrible concubinage; and that is why the wrath of God has fallen upon these sons of infidelity …

As part of their initiation ceremony, Templars were said to spit upon the crucifix.

The Grand Inquisitor of France, Guillaume de Paris, in collaboration with Philippe's chief minister, Guillaume de Nogaret, sent secret messengers to every royal bailiff and seneschal throughout the country, and at daybreak on 13 October the unsuspecting Templars were rounded up and flung into prison. Philippe also sent letters to other rulers inviting them to follow his example. In England, arrests took place on 10 January 1308; in Sicily on 24 January; and in Cyprus on 27 May. But in Spain the Templars held out for some time in their strongholds, and were not finally defeated until 2 November.

Historians have argued for centuries about the truth and significance of the charges against the Templars of 'odious rites' and sodomy. The rumour of the kiss 'at the base of the spine' was one that a rival order, the Hospitallers, had delighted in spreading; but the kiss on the mouth, the 'kiss of peace', was a common greeting during the Middle Ages. More sinister was the allegation that the belts worn by the

Templars, which they were supposed never to remove, had been consecrated to a heathen idol, in the shape of a bearded human head said to be called Baphomet, which was kissed and worshipped. But most significant is the fact that Philippe, who was very short of money and in great debt to the Templars, immediately took possession of all of their property.

The orders sent to the bailiffs and seneschals instructed them to appoint:

> … worthy and influential men, free from suspicion, knights, magistrates, and councillors, and inform them secretly under oath of their task and the information the King has received from the Pope and Church; and immediately they are to be sent to arrest the persons in each place, to seize their goods and arrange for their custody …
>
> Then they will place the persons, separately under good and safe guard, and make preliminary inquiries of them; next they will summon the Inquisitors' commissioners and investigate the truth carefully, using torture if necessary. And if they confess the truth, they will consign their depositions to writing, having summoned witnesses …
>
> Exhortations will be addressed to them relative to the articles of faith, and they will be told of the information laid before the Pope and King by several reliable witnesses, members of the order, of the error and buggery of which they render themselves especially guilty on entering the order, and of their declaration; and they will be promised a free pardon if they confess the truth on returning to the Faith of the Holy Church, or else they will be condemned to death. They will be asked under oath, carefully and judiciously, how they were received, what vows and promises they made, and they will be questioned in general terms until the truth is extracted from them, and they are prepared to persevere in it.

his feet were so badly burnt that the bones of his heel fell out a few days later

Some details of the tortures that the Templars endured have survived. Bernard de Gué had his feet so badly burnt by the inquisitors of Albi that the bones of his heel fell out a few days later. Ponsard de Gisy described how for three months: '… he was put in a dungeon, his hands tied behind his back so tightly that it caused the blood to run down his fingernails, and that he was left there, unable to stretch out …'.

In such conditions, 36 of the imprisoned Templars died in Paris, and another 25 in Sens – nobody knows how many died in other prisons.

It is not surprising that in most cases the inquisitors obtained the confessions they desired. Of 138 Templars arrested in Paris, only four denied the charges. All the others admitted denying Christ and spitting on the cross; and some three-quarters of these also admitted to the indecent kisses. But only half confessed to having been instructed in sodomy, and only a very few admitted to having seen the bearded idol Baphomet, whose existence was important to the charge of heresy.

One of these was the Templar Visitor of France, Hugues de Pairaud; this accorded with the belief that only the senior members of the order knew of the idol. He described it as a sort of sphinx, with four feet. Some more junior Templars were persuaded by the torturers to come up with descriptions, which varied considerably: Guillaume de Herblay said it was made of wood, covered with gold and silver; Jean du Tour claimed it was no more than a face painted on a wooden panel; but Raoul de Gizy was said to have described it as 'terrible – it seemed like the face of a demon. Each time he looked at it, he was so terrified he had to avert his eyes, trembling in every limb!'

Even the Grand Master, Jacques de Molay, admitted denying Christ and spitting

Even the Grand Master, Jacques de Molay, admitted denying Christ and spitting – although he claimed that he had spat only on the ground. He and the other three seniors of the order – Hugues de Pairaud, Geoffroy de Gonneville, and Geoffroy de Charnay – demanded to be heard personally by the pope. However, in April 1310 – after the arrested Templars, at least those who survived, had been in prison for 30 months – Philippe persuaded the pope to appoint Philippe de Marigny, the 22-year-old brother of one of his ministers, to the see of Sens, and the new archbishop promptly summoned his council to deliver judgment. Those who had stood by their original confessions were offered liberty, provided they were reconciled to the Church; but 54, who had revoked their confessions, were burned. As one chronicler put it, 'the courage they displayed at the stake placed their souls in great peril, for it led the common people into the error of believing them innocent'.

All over France, further holocausts followed. In 1312, the order was dissolved by papal decree. Finally, in 1314, the four leaders of the order were carried to the public scaffold in Paris to hear their sentences of life imprisonment proclaimed. Hugues de Pairaud and Geoffroy de Gonneville heard their condemnation in silence; but Jacques de Molay suddenly spoke out, declaring that the rule of the Templars had always been holy and righteous and Catholic, and it was innocent of the heresies of which it had been accused. As for himself, he deserved to die because, from fear of further torture, he had falsely admitted the accusations. Geoffroy de Charnay supported him. Both men were committed to the stake forthwith; the site of their execution, on the Ile de la Cité in Paris, is commemorated with a plaque.

In other countries the Templars were, on the whole, treated less harshly. In Germany, on the pope's dissolution of the order, they found refuge in the Order of St John, or in the Teutonic Knights. In Portugal they were cleared, and changed their name to the Knights of Christ. In England a royal warrant was issued in 1310 to permit the torture of arrested Templars, but their examiners complained at a lack of success. Eventually, most were consigned to monasteries to achieve reconciliation, and pensions were even provided for their subsistence. In Scotland only two Templars were ever arrested.

The Inquisition gains in strength

For over three centuries the sadistic, though relatively crude, forms of torture that have been described above were employed by the Inquisition, but the use of specifically designed instruments, such as the rack, the thumbscrews, or the 'Spanish boot' (see Chapter 8, page 134), was largely practised by the civil authorities, or by the Spanish Inquisition (also operating in Portugal), which was a separate organization, not under papal control.

Jacques de Molay, the Grand Master of the Templars. On the day of his execution in 1314, he declared that the Order was innocent of the heresies attributed to it.

However, the rules originally laid down were extended as the battle against heresy (which included Protestantism) increased in fervour during the second half of the fifteenth century and throughout the sixteenth. Torture was carried out for longer periods, and repeated. Originally, the progressive degrees of torture had been related to the seriousness of the charges against the accused, and might be seen as sufficient punishment in themselves. The victims could be considered as having purged their sins by their suffering. But the inquisitors soon became obsessed with the need to obtain a confession at all costs, and suspected heretics could count on the torture being continued until they told their tormentors what they wanted to hear.

Nevertheless, it was traditionally held that confessions obtained by torture were not legally acceptable, and that they must be confirmed by the victim within 24 hours, and in a place other than the torture chamber. The question arose as to what should be done with prisoners who thereupon withdrew their confessions. To solve this problem, a devious legal formula had been put forward by Nicolas Eymeric:

although torture should not be *repeated*, it could be *continued* – on a second day, or even a third, if necessary.

Even worse was the torture of those already found guilty, in order to extract the names of their accomplices, and of witnesses. However, as heretics were considered 'traitors against God's Majesty', this could be justified as the acceptable procedure in a trial for treason.

The penalty for treason was inevitably death; but the death commonly reserved for condemned heretics was burning at the stake. Logical reasons were put forward for this. The heretic held his unacceptable opinions in his mind, and expressed them by bodily actions; but his eternal soul might remain uncorrupted. This was equally true of those who were believed to be possessed by the Devil or one of his minions. It could be argued, therefore, that the only way of saving the heretic from God's punishment in the afterlife was to destroy his corrupted body and mind, and so free his soul, purged of all sin.

The setting-up of the machinery of the Inquisition, the involvement of the civil powers in what was originally a religious investigation, and the legalization of torture – not only to obtain a confession, but extended to get the accused to name accomplices – produced a powerful instrument of social terror. Moreover, the Church's justification of torture in cases of heresy made it easier for the secular courts to revive its use in the investigation of almost any type of crime. The example set by the

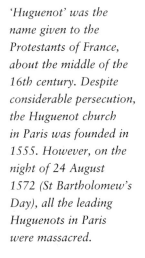

'Huguenot' was the name given to the Protestants of France, about the middle of the 16th century. Despite considerable persecution, the Huguenot church in Paris was founded in 1555. However, on the night of 24 August 1572 (St Bartholomew's Day), all the leading Huguenots in Paris were massacred.

Inquisition was eagerly followed by the civil authorities. And nowhere was it practised more cruelly, and senselessly, than in the European persecution of witches (see Chapter 7).

The Roman Inquisition

The rise of Protestantism set off the great witch hunts, and the worst excesses were committed, ironically, in Protestant territories. The Catholic Church had initiated the struggle against witchcraft as a heresy, but in 1542 Pope Paul III realized that official Protestantism represented a formidable danger to his power. With much of Italy under Spanish rule he had the example of the Spanish Inquisition before him: he therefore established a Roman Inquisition, specifically to root out Protestant heresy within the Vatican States, but effectually, since the pope was head of the whole Catholic world, as the ultimate authority in matters of faith.

the only way of saving the heretic was to destroy his corrupted body and mind

Six cardinals, the Congregation of the Inquisition, controlled the organization; they were authorized to appoint delegates, and to hear appeals against the sentences of these delegates. Under Paul III and his successor, Julius III, the Roman Inquisition acted with relative moderation, and Julius even ruled that its authority should be restricted to Italy alone. However, this situation changed markedly when Paul IV was elected in 1555. According to *The History of the Popes*:

> The hasty and credulous pope lent a willing ear to every denunciation, even the most absurd. Neither rank nor dignity nor merit weighed in the balance in the case of anyone suspected of heresy; he would be treated by the Inquisition as if he were the open and declared enemy of the Church. The inquisitors, constantly urged on by the pope, scented heresy in numerous cases where a calm and circumspect observer would not have discovered a trace of it ...

Paul IV was succeeded by Pius V, who was a Dominican and a former Grand Inquisitor. His aim was the elimination of heresy, false doctrine and error, and it is said that he often took a personal part in the activities of the Inquisition, urging the total destruction of the Huguenots in France and the Netherlands.

After Protestantism had been successfully suppressed in Italy, the Roman Inquisition concerned itself principally with the maintenance of the Catholic faith. In 1908, the name of Inquisition was dropped, and the organization became known solely as the Holy Office; and in 1965 this name was changed again, into the Congregation for the Doctrine of the Faith.

Chapter Four

Crude Methods of Torture

Since the primary principle of torture is to inflict pain – or, at the very least, to threaten pain, and so exploit the fear of it – the methods employed by the torturer can be of the crudest type: any form of violence is sufficient for his purpose. It is only when the legal code requires the form of torture, and its stages, to be strictly defined – or, alternatively, when the torturer derives particular sadistic pleasure from his duties – that special instruments and machines, such as those described in Chapter 8, have been devised.

The non-instrumental forms of torture used throughout many centuries can be divided into four classes; three of these involve the brutal use of physical force, fire, or water. The fourth class, which is best (if ironically) described as 'subtle' or 'refined' torture, can take a variety of forms, from the use of a caged biting insect (Chapter 3, page 44 and Chapter 9, page 155), or the Chinese bastinado (Chapter 9, page 148), to crude electric shock treatment (Chapter 8, pages 144–5), and purely psychological methods (Chapter 12).

The use of physical force can be further subdivided: into blows with a blunt instrument, cuts or pricks with a sharp implement, stretching and twisting, compression, and mutilation.

The more brutal torturers seldom employed just a single one of these methods. The lengths to which a torturer could go are exemplified in a speech made by Edmund Burke during the trial of Warren Hastings, who was charged in 1788 with violation of the trust reposed in him as Governor-General of India. One of Hastings's minions was a tax collector named Devi Sing:

> Those who could not raise the money were most cruelly tortured: cords were drawn tight round their fingers, till the flesh of the four on each hand was actually incorporated, and became one solid mass: the fingers were then separated again by wedges of iron and wood driven between them. Others were tied two and two by the feet, and thrown across a wooden bar, upon which they hung, with their feet uppermost; they were then beat on the soles of the feet, till their toenails dropped off. They

Irish-born Edmund Burke, a leading British politician during the second half of the 18th century, was critical of the corrupt government of India under the East India Company. He was responsible for the impeachment of the Governor-General, Warren Hastings, in 1788. In an impassioned speech, Burke described the brutal tortures that took place under Hastings's rule.

*'What modesty in
all nations most
carefully conceals,
this monster
revealed to view,
and consumed by
slow fires ...'*

were afterwards beat about the head till the blood gushed out at the mouth, nose and ears; they were also flogged upon the naked body with bamboo canes, and prickly bushes, and, above all, with some poisonous weeds, which were of a most caustic nature, and burnt at every touch.

The cruelty of the monster who had ordered all this, had contrived how to tear the mind as well as the body; he frequently had a father and son tied naked to one another by the feet and arms, and then flogged till the skin was torn from the flesh; and he had the devilish satisfaction to know that every blow must hurt; for if one escaped the son, his sensibility was wounded by the knowledge he had that the blow had fallen on his father: the same torture was felt by the father, when he knew that every blow that missed him had fallen on his son.

The treatment of the females could not be described ... the virgins were carried to the Court of Justice, where they might naturally have looked for protection, but now they looked for it in vain; for in the face of the Ministers of Justice, in the face of the spectators, in the face of the sun, those tender and modest virgins were brutally violated ... Other females had the nipples of their breasts put in a cleft bamboo, and torn off. What modesty in all nations most carefully conceals, this monster revealed to view, and consumed by slow fires ...

Crudely brutal methods such as these were employed over many centuries by the torturers of history, and sadly they continue to this day. The files of Amnesty International (Chapter 13, pages 186–7) are packed with reports of similar victims. For example, a Burmese student held by police officers in Mandalay in 1987 reported:

A team came in, stripped us of all our clothes ... tied up our hands with handcuffs and hung us up to the ceiling with a rope ... They interrogated me again and asked the same questions, to which I gave the same answers. So they whipped me with a car's fan belt ... Altogether I may have been given 70 or 80 lashes ... after a while I lost consciousness completely. They 'treated' my wounds the same way they treated my friend's ... they took him down, poured salt and curry powder on his back ... and then urinated on his back.

The tortures of stretching and compression have been dealt with in detail in other chapters, describing the rack and the *peine forte et dure* (see Chapter 8, pages 123–7 and Chapter 6, pages 85–7). Breaking on the wheel, a terrible punishment that inevitably resulted in death, was employed in many European countries, and particularly in France.

This wheel resembled a large cartwheel, about 2m (7ft) in diameter, mounted horizontally on a post. The victim was tied spread-eagled, either to the spokes or to the rim; the executioner then took an iron bar, a sledgehammer, or a heavy club, and smashed each limb in two places.

After this, it was customary to administer the *coup de grâce* with a blow to the neck or the stomach, but sometimes the victim was not so fortunate. When 86-year-old Jean Calas of Toulouse was accused of having arranged the strangulation of his own son in 1761, he was sentenced to be tortured, and then 'broken alive upon the wheel, to receive the last stroke after he had lain two hours, and then to be burnt to ashes'. In Germany, as many as 40 blows could be struck. One of the Nuremberg executioners is said to have been given the duty of administering the punishment to his own brother-in-law; it was reported that he gave him 'two tweaks with the red-hot tongs, [and] delivered 31 blows with the iron bar before despatching him'.

Breaking on the wheel. A form of punishment that was widely employed in Europe, and particularly in France. It inevitably resulted in the death of the victim.

'the hangman,
with a knife like
a gardener's
pruning knife, cut
off his ears'

The punishment of the wheel does not seem to have been used in England, but there are a few records of its use in Scotland. John Diksoun was executed for parricide in this way on 30 April 1591; and an entry in the diary of Robert Birrel records: 'Robert Weir broken on ane cartwheel … for murdering the Laird of Warriston, quilk he did, 2 Julii 1600'.

A punishment almost as brutal, although seldom fatal, was mutilation. Since most crimes, particularly those of theft or forgery, are committed with the hands, a typical sentence was to have one or both amputated. In London in 1581, John Stubs, the author of a pamphlet considered insulting to Elizabeth I, and his printer William Pace suffered similarly. On a scaffold in Westminster, 'their right hands were struck off, and a cleaver driven through the wrist with a beetle [hammer]'. When the bloody stumps had been cauterized with a hot iron, Pace cried, 'I have left here a true Englishman's hand', while Stubs waved his hat with his one remaining hand and shouted 'God save Queen Elizabeth!'

As with branding (see below), the purpose of mutilation was so that everyone could see, for the rest of the victim's life, that he had been convicted of a crime. In England during the sixteenth and seventeenth centuries many eminent persons lost part or all of their ears for seditious remarks. When Sir Robert Strange threatened the life of the Duke of Buckingham in 1628, he was whipped the length of the Strand from Temple Bar to Westminster, and there lost both ears, and was branded on the cheek.

As late as 1731, Sir Peter Stringer, 'who was, some time since, convicted of forging deeds of conveyance of 2000 acres [809 hectares] of land', was first placed in the pillory at Charing Cross:

The time being nearly expired, he was set on an elbow chair in the middle of the platform, when the hangman John Cooper … came up behind him and, with a knife like a gardener's pruning knife, cut off his ears and held them up so that the mob could see them. Having handed them to Mr Watson, the Sheriff's Officer, the hangman slit both nostrils with a pair of scissors …

The penalty for blasphemy was frequently to have the tongue torn out. In January 1535 a French Huguenot, Antoine Poile, had his tongue pierced and nailed to his cheek before he was burnt alive. In 1766, the Chevalier de la Barre, aged 17, was accused of damaging a wooden crucifix on the bridge at Abbeville. For this crime – or perhaps because he was an enthusiast for the works of Voltaire – he was tortured, and had his tongue cut out.

Mutilation was, and still is, widely practised in the Middle East. In his book *The History of Women* (1779), W. Alexander wrote of the Egyptians:

> The chastity of virgins was protected by a law of the severest nature; he who had committed a rape on a free woman had his privities cut off, that it might be out of his power ever to perpetrate the like crime, and that others might be terrified by so dreadful a punishment.

Torture by heat and fire

The pain of burning is perhaps the most acute of any. Over the centuries torturers have devised a variety of ways to exploit this. Some, such as the brazen bull, the boots or the Spanish chair (see Chapter 1, page

Torture of Dutch Catholics in the southern Netherlands in the late 16th century. The victim was laid on his back, with a large dish, containing several dormice, upturned on his naked belly. When a fire was lit on the dish, 'the dormice ... burrowed into the entrails of the victim'.

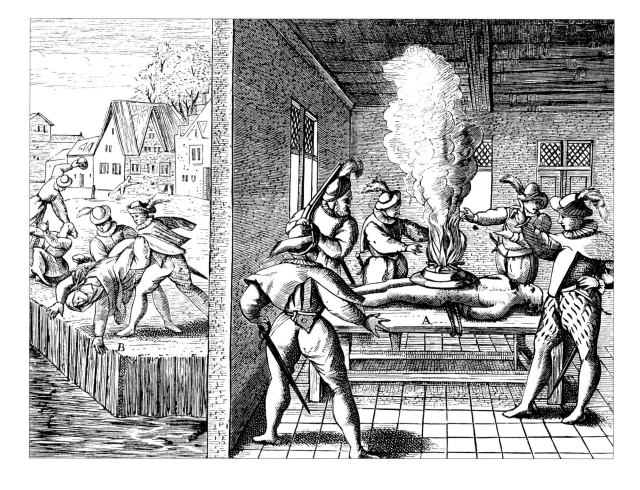

*Branding in the hand.
Rogues and vagabonds
were marked with
an 'R'; thieves with a
'T'; and those guilty
of manslaughter
with an 'M'.*

17, Chapter 8, pages 131–4, and Chapter 5, page 72), were specifically designed instruments of torture; but in most cases the agony of heat and fire was sufficient in its crudest form.

We have seen, in Chapter 3, how the trial by ordeal, in which the truth of litigants could be tested by their submission to the red-hot iron, led to the interrogative techniques of the Inquisition. Torturers of the Middle Ages took up the idea, and one method which was employed throughout Europe was the use of red-hot pincers.

When James I of Scotland was murdered in 1437, the principal conspirator was Walter, Earl of Atholl, who was a claimant to the throne. Walter was taken to the place of execution, the Cross in Edinburgh, and there his flesh was torn with pincers heated in a glowing brazier. An iron crown, taken from the fire, was then placed on his head, and he was proclaimed King of Traitors.

A similar fate was suffered in the Netherlands in 1584 by Balthasar Gerards, who had murdered William, Prince of Orange. After he had been flogged and racked, his body was ripped apart piece by piece with red-hot irons until he expired.

For lesser crimes, the penalty was not death, but branding. In England, miscreants were generally branded on the fleshy part of the left hand with the hot iron. Rogues and vagabonds were marked with the letter 'R'; thieves with 'T'; and those guilty of manslaughter with 'M'. Other parts of the body were also branded: for shoplifting, the cheek was burned; for blasphemy, the tongue was bored through with a red-hot skewer; for perjury, the letter 'P' was branded on the forehead.

Such penalties were laid down in a statute of 1548, and in 1624 the punishment was extended to women:

... be it enacted by the authority of this present Parliament, that any
woman being lawfully convicted by her confession, or by the verdict of
12 men, of or for the felonious taking of any money, goods, or chattels,
above the value of 12 pence, and under the value of 10 shillings; or as
accessory to any such offence; the said offence not being burglary, nor
robbery in or near the highway ... shall, for the first offence, be branded
and marked in the hand, upon the brawn of the thumb, with a hot
burning iron, having a roman T upon the said iron; ...

Branding remained a penalty in the English civil court until 1829, but
was not abolished in the army until 1879.

It was not only thieves and vagabonds who could suffer branding,
but also men of letters. In 1628 Alexander Leighton, a Scottish preacher,
was charged with 'framing, publishing and dispersing a scandalous book
directed against his King, peers and prelates'. He had one ear cut off,
and his face was branded with the letters 'SS', for 'sower of sedition'.
And in 1637, William Prynne, an English barrister and MP who had
already lost both ears on account of his writings, was branded and
sentenced to be imprisoned for life for publishing pamphlets attacking
the bishops of the Church of England. The letters 'SL' – for 'schismatic
libeller' – were burned, one into each cheek.

In France, the brand mark was at first the *fleur de lis*. Later this was
replaced by the letters 'TF', indicating *travaux forces* – hard labour.
A different punishment was ordained for the Comtesse Jeanne de
La Motte Valois. In 1786 she stole and sold a magnificent diamond
necklace that Louis XV had ordered, before his death, for his mistress
Madame du Barry. She was sentenced to be birched naked in public, and
then branded on each shoulder with the letter 'V', for *voleuse* (thief).
However, after one shoulder had been marked she twisted violently, and
the hot iron fell on her naked breast.

Cruder methods were also used. A 1624 account of an interrogation
by the Dutch in the East Indies described how:

... they hoisted him up againe as before, and then burnt him with lighted
candles in the bottome of his feete, untill the fat dropt out the candles;
yet then applied they fresh lights unto them. They burnt him also under
the elbowes, and in the palmes of the hands; likewise under the arme-
pitts, until his inwards might evidently be seene.

Such cruelty, although officially outlawed, has continued into the
twentieth century. For the past 100 years, many police officers have
had the means of torture readily available in their pockets: cigarettes

*He had one ear
cut off, and his
face was branded
with the letters
'SS', for 'sower
of sedition'*

and lighters. In 1990, Sehmus Ukus, a Turkish Kurd, was arrested in Greece. He claimed that the police had cuffed his hands behind his back, and then burned the soles of his feet and his genitals with a cigarette lighter before beating him. When a senior officer asked why he was being beaten, the answer was 'He is a Turk'. In 1991, Indian shopkeeper Manzoor Ahmed Naikoo reported of his captors how 'after tying me down, they removed my pyjamas. They tied cloth to my penis and set it on fire.'

An earlier torture was roasting alive on a gridiron. This was the martyrdom of St Lawrence, put to death by the Romans in AD 258. It is said that as he lay in agony he called out to the executioner: 'This side is roasted enough; decide whether roasted or raw thou thinkest the better meat!'

There were other ways of exploiting heat in torture: boiling water, oil or tallow, or molten lead were often employed. Usually these were only a part of the torture, but they might also be used as a final punishment. In England in 1531, Richard Roose poisoned 17 members of the Bishop of Rochester's household, two of whom died. A special Act of

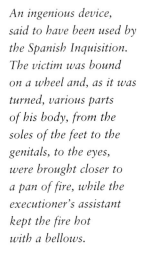

An ingenious device, said to have been used by the Spanish Inquisition. The victim was bound on a wheel and, as it was turned, various parts of his body, from the soles of the feet to the genitals, to the eyes, were brought closer to a pan of fire, while the executioner's assistant kept the fire hot with a bellows.

Parliament was passed, by which he was sentenced to be 'boyled to deathe withoute havynge any advauntage of clergie'. The Act remained on the Statute Book for 16 years, and in 1541 a maidservant, Margaret Dawe, suffered the same fate for a similar crime.

Water torture

Water is generally so readily available, and so easily handled, that torturers have used it in a wide variety of ways for many centuries. The simplest of all is to force the victim to drink: at first this comes as a welcome relief after the pains that have gone before; but then the victim becomes sated, bloated, and soon in intense discomfort. The effects were dramatically described by William Lithgow, a Scot who was mistaken for a spy in Spain in 1620. After he had been racked:

> ... the tormentor ... went to an earthen jar standing full of water, a little beneath my head; from whence carrying a pot full of water, in the bottom whereof there was an incised hole, which being stopped by his thumb, till it came to my mouth, he did pour it in my belly; the measure being a Spanish *sombre* which is an English pottle; the first and second devices I gladly received, such was the scorching drought of my tormenting pain, and likewise I had drunk none for three days before.
>
> But afterward, at the third charge perceiving these measures of water to be inflicted on me as tortures, O strangling tortures! I closed my lips again-standing that eager crudelity. Whereat the *Alcaide* [governor of the prison] enraged, set my teeth asunder with a pair of iron cadges, detaining them there, at every several turn, both mainly and manually; whereupon my hunger-clunged belly waxing great, grew drum-like imbolstred, for it being a suffocating pain, in regard of my head hanging downward, and the water reingorging itself, in my throat, with a struggling force, it strangled and swallowed up my breath from yowling and groaning.

A sadistic refinement of this method was used by the Dutch at Amboyna, in the East Indies, during the interrogation of a number of English merchants who were suspected of plotting to capture the Dutch headquarters in 1622:

> Then they bound a cloth about his necke and face so close that little or no water could go by. That done, they poured the water softly upon his head untill the cloth was full, up to the mouth and nostrills, and somewhat higher; so that he could not draw breath, but he must withall suck-in the water ... which being still continued to be poured in softly,

'it strangled and swallowed up my breath from yowling and groaning'

forced all his inward parts, came out of his nose, eares, and eyes, and often as it were stifling and choaking him, at length took away his breath, and brought him to a swounce or fainting.

Then they tooke him quickly downe, and made him vomit up the water. Being a little recovered, they triced him up againe, poured in the water as before, eftsoones taking him downe as he seemed to be stifled. In this manner they handled him three or four severall times with water, till his body was swolne twice or thrice as bigge as before, his cheekes like great bladders, and his eyes staring and strutting out beyond his forehead ...

prisoners could see each drop coming and were gradually driven frantic

Yet another variation of this water torture, which was also empl-oyed by the Dutch, is described by the seventeenth-century writer Ernestus Eremundus Frisius in his book *The History of the Low Countries' Disturbances*:

There is a bench, which they call the wooden horse, made hollow like a trough, so as to contain a man lying on his back at full length, about the middle of which there is a round bar laid across, upon which the back of the person is placed, so that he lies upon the bar instead of being let down into the bottom of the trough, with his feet much higher than his head.

As he is lying in this posture, his arms, thighs, and shins are tied round with small cords or strings which, being drawn with screws at proper distances from each other, cut into his very bones, so as to be no longer discerned. Besides this, the torturer throws over his mouth and nostril a thin cloth, so that he is scarcely able to breathe thro' them, and in the mean while a small stream of water like a thread, not drop by drop, falls from on high, upon the mouth of the person lying in this miserable condition, and so easily sinks down the thin cloth to the bottom of his throat, so that there is no possibility of breathing, his mouth being stopped with water and his nostrils with the cloth, so that the poor wretch is in the same agony as persons ready to die, and breathing out their last.

When this cloth is drawn out of his throat, as it often is, so that he may answer to the questions, it is all wet with water and blood, and is like pulling his bowels through his mouth.

Hippolytus de Marsiliis, the sixteenth-century lawyer (see Chapter 3, pages 43–4), is credited with the invention of a particularly subtle form of water torture. Having observed how drops of water falling one by one on a stone gradually wore away a hollow, he applied the method to the human body. Victims were strapped down so that they could not move, and cold water was then dripped slowly on to a small

The water torture. A piece of cloth was laid over the victim's mouth and nostrils. A stream of water was poured on to it, forcing the cloth down into the prisoner's throat, so that he was unable to breathe.

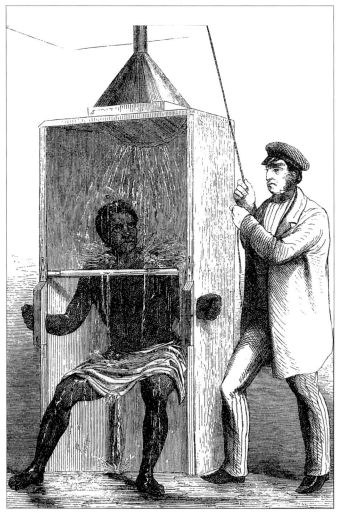

A common punishment used in American prisons during the 19th century. A troublesome convict would be locked into a cubicle, and subjected to a shower of ice-cold water.

area of the body. The forehead was found to be the most suitable point for this form of torture: prisoners could see each drop coming, and were gradually driven frantic.

An alternative was to pour a continuous stream of water from a height on to the victim's forehead. Similar to this was the treatment that was meted out in American prisons in the nineteenth century: a troublesome convict would be locked into a shower cubicle under a spray of ice-cold water. Such a punishment could prove fatal – in 1858 Simon Moore, an inmate of Auburn prison, New York State, collapsed and died after half an hour in these conditions, and in 1882 all cold water torture was abolished in American prisons.

In the present century, interrogators have largely given up these more ingenious tortures, and settled for the simple expedient of immersing the victim in a bath of cold water (see Chapter 11, pages 164–5). A recent case was reported by a Paraguayan prisoner:

In the centre of the room there was an ordinary bathtub, rather large. From a hole in the wall hung a plastic pipe from which water was flowing to fill the bath ... They made me sit down on the edge of the trough at its highest part, having first tied my feet with ropes and my hands behind my back ...

Suddenly they grabbed me by the shoulders and pushed me to the bottom of the trough. I held my breath a while, making desperate efforts to get my head out of the water and take in some air. I managed to free my head but they submerged me again, and when my efforts to get out became violent, the heaviest members of the group trampled on the top part of my body. I could no longer bear the lack of air, and began to swallow water through my mouth, nose, and ears.

My ears started to hum as the water made its way in. They seemed to be blowing up like a balloon. Then came a sharp whistling, very loud at first, which has not yet completely gone, and which I hear when there is complete silence. The more I swallowed water the more my struggles to breathe also increased, and they all pressed me down to the bottom of the trough – my head, chest, and hands ... I must have swallowed 8 to 10 litres of water. When they took me out and laid me on the ground, one of them trod heavily on my stomach; water poured out from my mouth and nose, spurting like a jet from a hose.

In Spanish- and Portuguese-speaking countries – the Philippines, Bolivia, Uruguay, Brazil, Paraguay, and Mexico – this treatment is jocularly described by the torturers as *el submarino*. A different technique has also been reported from Mexico. Known as the *Tehuacanazo*, it takes its name from a popular brand of mineral water; the effervescent liquid is forced into the victim's nostrils, and sometimes mixed with chilli powder.

Finally, mention must be made of an inhuman punishment practised in the Royal Navy for nearly two centuries. It is described in a publication of 1634:

> The ducking att the maine yarde arme is, when a malefactor by having a rope fastened under his armes and about his middle, and under his breech, is thus hoysted up to the end of the yarde; from whence hee is violentlie let fall into the sea, sometimes twise, sometimes three severall tymes one after another; and if the offence be very fowle, he is alsoe drawn under the very keele of the shippe, the which is termed keel-rakinge; and while hee is thus under water, a great gunn is given fire unto righte over his head; the which is done as well to astonish him the more with the thunder thereof, which muche troubles him, as to give warning untoe all others to looke out, and to beware by his harmes.

The ducking-stool (see page 137) was a particularly English form of water torture. It was customarily imposed as a punishment for scolding women.

Chapter Five

The Spanish Inquisition

Few legal institutions have earned a worse reputation, or inspired more fear, than the Inquisition in Spain. Yet, compared with such events in most of southern Europe, it had a relatively late development. While the fight against heresy went on in other parts of Europe during the thirteenth century, the inhabitants of Christian Spain had a more pressing concern. The struggle against Moorish occupation was long and hard, and served to strengthen their faith. It was only as the reconquest of the peninsula was gradually completed that the question of the need for religious unity within the kingdom was raised.

At first, the Jews were regarded as the principal obstruction to this aim. They had been tolerated under Moorish rule: scholars and merchants, they had grown in numbers and influence for seven centuries. And so, in the late fourteenth century, Henry III of Castile and Leon began to exert pressure on the Jewish community: they were given the alternatives of baptism into the Christian faith, or death.

Those who openly converted from Judaism, but frequently continued to practise their religion in secret, were known as *marranos* – an unfortunate name that more commonly meant 'filthy swine'. It has been calculated that there were more than 100,000 of them, and when Castile and Aragon were united in 1469 by the marriage of Ferdinand and Isabella (the 'Catholic kings'), these *marranos* were declared a danger to the faith in Spain, and so to the safety of the kingdom.

In 1478 Pope Sixtus IV was persuaded to issue a bull that authorized the Catholic kings to name the inquisitors they wished to be appointed. This was intended to be an alliance of Church and State, but in reality it resulted in a strengthening of the absolute power of the throne. The earliest Spanish inquisitors, who set themselves up in Seville, showed such zeal in the pursuit of heresy that the pope attempted to restrain them; but the Spanish Government now realized what a powerful weapon they had in their hands, and Sixtus found that he was unable to influence them. In 1483 he was compelled to agree to the appointment of Inquisitors General for Castile and Leon; Aragon, Valencia, and Catalonia came under the control of the Inquisition during the same year.

(Opposite) An 18th-century impression of tortures employed by the Spanish Inquisition, including the strappado, the use of fire on the soles of the feet, and the water torture. The chief inquisitor sits at the back of the room, and a clerk in front of him takes down the answers to his interrogation.

*The Dominican priest
Tomás de Torquemada
was the first Grand
Inquisitor of the Spanish
Inquisition, appointed
in 1483. He pursued a
campaign of persecution
against the murranos,
Jews who agreed to
become Christians, but
secretly continued
to practise their
own religion.*

The Inquisitors General for these five kingdoms were supervised by a Grand Inquisitor; he was appointed by the government, and Rome was forced to give him judicial authorization. Assisted by his council of five, he had the power to appoint deputies and hear appeals.

The first Grand Inquisitor was the Dominican priest Tomás de Torquemada, 'whose name has come to symbolize all the worst aspects of the Spanish Inquisition, and to be a synonym for religious bigotry and cruel fanaticism'. He was appointed in August 1483, and set up tribunals in Seville, Jaén, Córdoba, Ciudad Real, and Zaragoza. The following year he drew up a document of 28 articles as a guide for the local inquisitors: they were to inquire not only into the crimes of heresy and apostasy, but also witchcraft, bigamy, blasphemy, and usury, and they were authorized to use torture in the obtaining of evidence.

Torquemada has been credited with persuading Ferdinand and Isabella (to whom he was confessor) to publish their edict of 31 March 1492, by which Spanish Jews were given the alternatives of conversion to Christianity, or banishment. As a result, over 160,000 Jews left Spain; most of these were Sephardic Jews, and their medieval Spanish survived into modern times, in the same way that Yiddish (*Jüdische deutsch*) survived among the German-speakers. Those who remained and accepted Christianity were known as *conversos*. Although Christopher Columbus is generally believed to have been born in Genoa, in Italy, he spoke only Spanish and called himself Cristobal Colón; the Spaniards claim him for their own, and some historians have suggested that he was, in fact, a converted Jew. Indeed, it has been said that Torquemada's own family were *conversos*.

This may explain the violence of Torquemada's campaign against the *conversos*. Several thousand were condemned to be burned at the stake for secretly practising their true religion. The entire family of the philosopher Juan Luis Vives – professor of humanities at Louvain, later doctor of laws at Corpus Christi, Oxford, and tutor to Henry VIII's daughter Mary – was exterminated in this manner.

One of the earlier victims of Torquemada's campaign was a certain Benito García. He had been a professed Christian for 35 years, and was returning home from a pilgrimage to the shrine of St James at Santiago de

Compostella, when he was arrested in June 1490. A consecrated wafer was found in his knapsack. In the course of six days of torture, he named five *conversos* and two Jews as his accomplices in the ritual murder of a child from the village of La Guardia. He said that they planned to use the child's heart and the wafer in a spell that would cause all Christians to die, and the Jews to come by their wealth. No child was ever reported as missing from La Guardia, but Torquemada gave such publicity to the allegations that, by autumn of the following year, a cult of the Holy Child of La Guardia had already been established.

However, many *conversos* survived and genuinely embraced Roman Catholicism, and in due course contributed immeasurably to the religious and intellectual life of Spain. At least two saints – Teresa of Avila and St John of God – have been claimed as coming from *converso* families, as has Diego Laínez, second general of the Jesuit order.

By the mid-sixteenth century, after two generations of *conversos*, the Inquisition was no longer principally concerned with the rooting out of Jewish religion, and turned its attention to the censorship of 'heretical' publications, and the enforcement of 'correct' religious beliefs among Christians – even Ignatius Loyola, the founder of the order of Jesuits, was twice arraigned for heresy. However, the Inquisition was instrumental in the dissemination of a new and pernicious doctrine, that of *limpieza* (purity). This was imposed on the cathedral chapter of Toledo, in 1547, by its archbishop; similar to the later racial laws of the Nazis, it required all future ecclesiastical appointees to prove the purity of their ancestry, free from any *converso* blood or accusations of heresy. The statute was approved in 1556 by King Philip II (husband of the English Queen Mary), who declared that 'all the heresies in Germany, France and Spain have been sown by descendants of the Jews'. Similar statutes were adopted throughout the Spanish world, and gave impetus to a further seeking-out of Jewish ancestry.

Spain's dominions at this time included the newly discovered lands in America and Sicily, the kingdom of Naples, and the Netherlands, and in 1580 Portugal also became part of Spain. All these territories, with the exception of Naples, whose inhabitants vehemently opposed it, were subject to the tortures of the Spanish Inquisition.

In 1554 the lawyer J. Damhouder described a typical torture by a crude means of racking, employed in Bruges, in the Spanish Netherlands:

> The victim is stripped naked and laid on a straight bench, his hands tied behind his back, his belly in the air. His genitals are covered with a linen cloth. He is tied down to the bench, under his armpits and round

He said that they planned to use the child's heart and the wafer in a spell

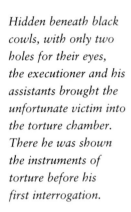

Hidden beneath black cowls, with only two holes for their eyes, the executioner and his assistants brought the unfortunate victim into the torture chamber. There he was shown the instruments of torture before his first interrogation.

his diaphragm, to prevent his falling off. His two big toes are tied to a cord, which stretches his body by means of a wheel, a stick, or similar instrument. Afterward, another cord may be tied above the knee round his thighs, which can be tightened, more or less, at the discretion of the judge … Sometimes a loop made of knotted rope, known as a *paternoster*, is tied round the head and forehead, tightened with two sticks or bones, according to the judge's discretion. Then the executioner may place a clean cloth over the sufferer's eyes and, forcing his nostrils closed with it, pours a jar over his diaphragm, calves, toes, and elsewhere, and then, forcing open his mouth with a small bridle, pours in cold water, until he swells up to the point where the judge and his council consider he can no longer endure it without the greatest peril …

The good judge is always compassionate, and must take into account the youth or age of the accused and the state of his health, to ensure that his office be that of the good judge, and not the bloodthirsty tyrant. He must start carefully and moderately, then rigorously, and finally very rigorously indeed, according to the gravity of the crime and the degree of proof against the accused, and the nature of his replies. He must take no notice of the screams, cries, sighs, tremblings, or pain of the accused; and all must be done with such care and moderation that the accused be neither driven mad, wounded, hurt, nor unduly distressed …

If this was the attitude of the 'good judge', we can imagine the torments endured by those in the hands of other, less scrupulous, inquisitors. And what could the avoidance of 'undue distress' mean, when every muscle in the accused's body was, in fact, being lawfully torn apart?

Unlike the courts of the Dominican inquisitors in France, Italy, and Germany, the courts of the Spanish Inquisition were specifically built, and were often magnificent palaces. In Portugal, for example, the house of the Inquisition contained four imposing courtrooms, a spacious set of apartments for the Inquisitor General, and suites of rooms surrounding a central courtyard, which were occupied by members of the royal court and other personages when they wished to view the executions that took place there.

The Inquisition's proceedings were held in secret, and the accused were denied representation by counsel, or the right to confront hostile witnesses. When they were condemned, their property was confiscated, and shared between the Inquisition, the Crown, and their accusers. The terror that the process inspired was great, even without the awesome threat of the underground torture chamber, where the executioner waited, clothed from head to toe in black, and with his face concealed in a black cowl, with only two holes for his eyes.

In his *History of the Inquisition* (1731), Philip van Limborch described what first happened there:

> The stripping is performed without regard to humanity or honour, not only to men, but to women and virgins, the most virtuous and chaste of whom they have sometimes in their prisons. For they cause them to be stripped, even to their very shifts, which they afterwards take off, forgive the expression, even to their pudenda, and then put on their strait linen drawers.

The first stage of torture was generally 'squassation', which was equivalent to the fourth degree of the strappado described by Grillandus (see Chapter 3, page 43): suspended face-downward from a rope tied to the arms behind the back, the victim was at intervals suddenly let down with a jerk, so that gradually all joints were dislocated. Following this, according to Frederic Shoberl:

> If this torture was not sufficient to overcome him, that of water was resorted to. He was obliged to swallow a great quantity, and then laid in a wooden trough, provided with a lid that might be pressed down as

'He must take no notice of the screams, cries, tremblings, or pain of the accused'

tight as the operators pleased. Across the trough was a bar, on which the sufferer's back rested, and by which the spine was broken.

The torture by fire was equally painful. A very brisk fire was made; and, the prisoner being extended on the ground, the soles of his feet were rubbed with lard or some other combustible matter, and placed close to the fire, till the agony extorted from him such a confession as his tormentors required.

One of the simplest, yet most effective, tortures employed by the Inquisition was to apply the heat of a fire to the soles of the victim's feet.

A fiendish development of this method was the 'Spanish chair'. This was a heavy iron structure in which the victim was seated, with straps around the neck, arms, and upper legs, his feet locked in a pair of iron stocks. A glowing brazier would be placed close to the feet, or beneath the seat, in order that its heat would gradually spread to all parts of the chair.

If these methods failed to break the victim's spirit, there was still the *potro*, or rack. This could take various forms, not always involving stretching the victim's body (see Chapter 8, pages 123–8). In Lisbon in

1753, for example, an Englishman, John Coustos, was fastened to the rack by his ankles, with a collar about his neck. Ropes were then wound around his arms and legs, and through holes in the frame, and gradually drawn tighter and tighter, so that they cut through his flesh to the bone.

In a curious book entitled *A Master Key to Popery*, written in 1725 by Antonio Gavin, some other distinctly unconventional and sadistic tortures are described. According to this account, when French troops captured the city of Aragon, the prisons of the Inquisition were opened, and some 400 prisoners were released. 'Among these were 60 beautiful young women who appeared to form a seraglio for the three principal inquisitors.' One of these related her experiences at the hands of Don Francisco Torregon, the second inquisitor, and told what she had been shown by one of the female servants:

> Taking me downstairs, she brought me to a large room, with a thick iron door, which she opened. Within it was an oven, with a fire in it at the time, and a large brass pan upon it, with a cover of the same, and a lock to it. In the next room there was a great wheel, covered on both sides with thick boards, with a little window in the centre; Mary desired me to look in with a candle; there I saw all the circumference of the wheel set with sharp razors, which made me shudder. Mary then took me to a pit, which was full of venomous animals.
>
> On my expressing great horror at the sight, she said, 'Now, my good mistress, I'll tell you the use of these things. The dry pan is for heretics, and those who oppose the holy father's will and pleasure; they are put alive into the pan, being first stripped naked; and the cover being locked down, the executioner begins to put a small fire into the oven, and by degrees he augments it, till the body is reduced to ashes. The wheel is designed for those who speak against the Pope, or the holy fathers of the Inquisition; for they are put into that machine through the little door, which is locked after them, and then the wheel is turned swiftly, till they are all cut to pieces. The pit is for those who contemn the images, and refuse to give proper respect to ecclesiastical persons; for they are thrown into the pit, and so become the food of poisonous animals.

This account is doubtful: the further experiences of the young captive savour too much of the sensational anti-Catholic fiction of the time.

Surprisingly, not all the victims satisfied their torturers by confessing; women seem to have been particularly steadfast. Engracia Rodríguez, 60 years old, remained obdurate, despite having an arm broken and a toe torn off. In Lisbon, Maria da Coceicao, a young woman accused of

'Among these were 60 beautiful young women who appeared to form a seraglio for the three principal inquisitors.'

*'The prisoners
who are to be
roasted alive have
a Jesuit on
each side'*

heresy, confessed on the rack, but later refused to sign the document ratifying her confession. Put to the rack again, she again confessed, but once more refused to sign, saying 'as soon as I am released from the rack I shall deny what was extorted from me by pain'. On a third racking, she refused to answer a single question. Defeated, the inquisitors ordered that she should be whipped publicly through the streets, and then banished for 10 years.

Those who in this way escaped execution were few, and they did not dare express criticism of what they had suffered. As Dellon put it in his *Account of the Inquisition at Goa* (1788):

> Those who have thus escaped the fire by their forced confessions, when they are put out of the prison of the Holy Office, are strictly obliged to publish that they were treated with much goodness and clemency, since their life was preserved to them, which they had justly forfeited. For if a man who having confessed himself guilty, should afterwards presume to justify himself after his enlargement [release], he would be immediately accused, arrested, and burnt at the first *Act of Faith*, without any hope of pardon.

This 'act of faith' was in Portuguese the *auto-da-fé*, the name by which it is generally known. It was a mass parade of the convicted victims, some of whom had been kept in prison for several years until there was a sufficient number to be punished in a great public ceremony, at the close of which 20 or 30 would be burned alive in the midst of an enthusiastic crowd. In *Faiths of the World* (1858), James Gardner quotes a certain Mr Dowling's eye-witness account:

> The victims who walk in the procession wear the *san benito*, the *coroza*, the rope around the neck, and carry in their hand a yellow wax candle. The *san benito* is a penitential garment or tunic of yellow cloth reaching down to the knees, and on it is painted the picture of the person who wears it, burning in the flames, with figures of dragons and devils in the act of fanning the flames. This costume indicates that the wearer is to be burnt alive as an incorrigible heretic.
>
> If the person is only to do penance, then the *san benito* has on it a cross, and no paintings or flames. If an impenitent is converted just before being led out, then the *san benito* is painted with the flames downward; this is called *fuego resuelto*, and indicates that the wearer is not to be burnt alive, but to have the favour of being strangled before the flame is applied to the pile. Formerly these garments were hung up

in the churches as eternal monuments of disgrace to their wearers, and as the trophies of the Inquisition.

The *coroza* is a pasteboard cap, three feet [90cm] high, and ending in a point. On it are likewise painted crosses, flames, and devils. In Spanish America it was customary to add long twisted tails to the *corozas*. Some of the victims have gags in their mouths, of which a number is kept in reserve in case the victims, as they march along in public, should become outrageous, insult the tribunal, or attempt to reveal any secrets.

The prisoners who are to be roasted alive have a Jesuit on each side continually preaching to them to abjure their heresies, and if any one attempts to offer one word in defence of the doctrines for which he is going to suffer death, his mouth is instantly gagged. 'This I saw done to a prisoner,' says Dr Geddes … 'presently after he came out of the gates of the Inquisition, upon his having looked up to the sun, which he had not seen before for several years, and cried out in a rapture, "How is it possible for people that behold that glorious body to worship any being but him that created it?"'

The banner of the Inquisition of the Portuguese colony of Goa, India. The prison there was described by Torres de Castilla as 'the dirtiest, darkest and most horrible that can possibly be, into which the rays of the sun never penetrate'.

The same Dr Geddes was witness to an *auto-da-fé* that took place in Madrid in 1682:

The officers of the Inquisition, preceded by trumpets, kettle-drums and their banner, marched on the 30th of May, in cavalcade, to the palace of the great square, where they declared by proclamation that on the 30th of June the sentence of the prisoners would be put in execution. There had not been a spectacle of this kind at Madrid for several years before, for which reason it was expected by the inhabitants with as much impatience as a day of the greatest festivity and triumph.

When the day appointed arrived … people appeared, dressed as splendidly as their respective circumstances would admit. In the great square was raised a high scaffold; and thither from seven in the morning till the evening, were brought criminals of both sexes; all the Inquisitions in the kingdom were sending their prisoners to Madrid.

Twenty men and women out of these prisoners, with one renegade Mahometan, were ordered to be burned; 50 Jews and Jewesses, having never before been imprisoned, and repenting of their crimes, were sentenced to a long confinement, and to wear a yellow cap; and ten others, indicted for bigamy, witchcraft and other crimes, were sentenced to be whipped and then sent to the galleys: these last wore large pasteboard caps, with inscriptions on them, having a halter about their necks, and torches in their hands.

On this solemn occasion the whole court of Spain was present. The Grand Inquisitor's chair was placed in a sort of tribunal far above that of the king. The nobles here acted the part of the sheriffs' officers in England, leading such criminals as were to be burned … the rest of the

A typical auto-da-fé. *The prisoners are dressed in a sort of smock, the* san benito, *with a high pasteboard cap, the* coroza, *on the head. Beside each one, Jesuits preach to him to abjure his heresy.*

criminals were conducted by the familiars of the Inquisition.

At the place of execution there are so many stakes set as there are prisoners to be burned, a large quantity of dry furze being set about them. The stakes of the Protestants, or, as the inquisitors call them, the professed, are about four yards [three and a half metres] high, and have each a small board, whereon the prisoner is seated within half a yard [45cm] of the top.

The professed then go up a ladder betwixt two priests, who attend them the whole day of execution. When they come even with the aforesaid board, they turn about to the people, and the priests spend near a quarter of an hour in exhorting them to be reconciled to the see of Rome. On their refusing, the priests come down, and the executioner ascending, turns the professed from off the ladder upon the seat, chains their bodies close to the stakes, and leaves them. Then the priests go up a second time to renew their exhortations; and if they find them ineffectual, usually tell them at parting, that 'they leave them to the Devil, who is standing at their elbow ready to receive their souls, and carry them with him into the flames of hell-fire, as soon as they are out of their bodies.'

A general shout is then raised, and when the priests get off the ladder, the universal cry is: 'Let the dogs' beards be made!' (which implies, singe their beards). This is accordingly performed by means of flaming furzes, thrust against their faces with long poles. This barbarity is repeated till their faces are burnt, and is accompanied with loud acclamations. Fire is then set to the furzes, and the criminals are consumed.

The intrepidity of the 21 men and women in suffering the horrid death was truly astonishing; some thrust their hands and feet into the flames with the most dauntless fortitude; and all of them yielded to their fate with such resolution that many of the amazed spectators lamented that such heroic souls had not been more enlightened. The near situation of the king to the criminals rendered their dying groans very audible to him; he could not, however, be absent from this dreadful scene, as it is esteemed a religious one, and his coronation oath obliges him to give a sanction by his presence to all the acts of the tribunal.

Historians dispute the number of victims burned at the stake. Llorente – for some years reportedly secretary to the Inquisition – estimated that between 1481 and 1517 at least 13,000 were burned alive, 8700 burnt in effigy (which meant they had been previously strangled in prison), and 17,000 condemned to various punishments. He also calculated that, from 1481 to 1808, a total of 341,021 were condemned to

'The intrepidity of the men and women suffering the horrid death was truly astonishing'

A grand auto-da-fé *before a royal audience, in the Plaza Mayor, Madrid. Prisoners of the Inquisition were brought from all over Spain to learn their punishment here, and crowds of richly-dressed people and nobles were present at what was regarded as the height of popular entertainment.*

death in Spain alone. Other authorities consider these numbers greatly exaggerated, so much so, that Torquemada, who was Grand Inquisitor from 1483 to 1498, has been accused – 'at a fair estimate' – of no more than 2000 deaths.

Nevertheless, there are records indicating the severe sentences pronounced upon many unfortunates, often for relatively trivial offences. Rochus, a wood-carver of San Lucar, was burned for defacing an image of the Virgin Mary, rather than sell it at the bargain price demanded by an inquisitor. A Protestant named Juan Léon, who tried, together with some companions, to escape to England, was tortured and burned. Another Protestant, the eminent physician Cristofero Losada, was racked and burned, as was a writing-master of Toledo, who decorated the walls of a room in his house with the ten commandments.

An Englishwoman, who was married to a Portuguese named Vasconcellos in Madeira, was accused of heresy in 1704, and sent to the Inquisition in Lisbon. There she was kept in prison for over nine months; she was flogged several times to persuade her to confess, and her breast was burnt in three places with a red-hot iron. At last, she was taken to the torture chamber and strapped into the Spanish chair; an iron slipper, heated in the fire until it was red hot, was placed on her left foot. The flesh was burnt to the bone, and she fainted. When she came to, she was once more flogged until her whole back was a mass of blood, and then threatened with the slipper on her other foot. Unsurprisingly, she signed her confession, and was eventually released.

For discussing Protestantism with a friend, Jane Bohorquia of Seville was put to the rack. She was pregnant at the time, and a week later she died. The Inquisition reported: 'Jane Bohorquia was found dead in prison; after which, upon reviewing her prosecution, the Inquisition discovered her innocent. Be it therefore known that no further prosecution shall be carried on against her ... '

In 1714 an Englishman, Isaac Martin, was seized in Malaga, under suspicion of being a Jew. He was taken before the Inquisition at Granada, and thrown into prison with these words: 'You must observe a great silence here as if you were dead; you must not speak, nor whistle, nor sing, nor make any noise that can be heard; and if you hear anybody cry, or make a noise, you must be still, and say nothing, upon pain of 200 lashes.' After a long imprisonment, he received notice of what his punishment was to be:

Jane Bohorquia of Seville was put to the rack. She was pregnant at the time, and a week later she died.

> The next morning, about ten of the clock, I was brought downstairs, the executioner came in with ropes and a whip. He bid me take off my coat, waistcoat, wig and cravat. As I was taking off my shirt, he bid me let it alone, he would manage that. He slipp'd my body through the collar, and ty'd it about my waist. Then took a rope and ty'd my hands together, put another about my neck, and led me out of the Inquisition, where there were numerous crowds of people waiting to see an English heretic.
>
> I was no sooner out, but a priest read my sentence at the door, as followeth: 'Orders are given from the Lords of the Holy Office of the Inquisition, to give unto Isaac Martin 200 lashes, through the public streets. He being of the religion of the Church of England, a Protestant, a Heretic, irreverend to the Host, and to the Image of the Virgin Mary, and so let it be executed.' ... The sentence being read, the executioner mounted me upon an ass, and led me through the streets, the people Huzzahing, and crying out, an English Heretic! Look at the English Heretic, who is no Christian, and pelting me. The cryer of the city walked before me, repeating aloud the sentence that was read at the door of the Inquisition, the executioner whipping me as I went along, and a

great many people on horseback, in ceremonial robes, with wands and halberds following.

The Inquisition was no respecter of persons. One of its victims was none other than Carlos, the eldest son of Philip II, and heir to the throne. Reputedly, Don Carlos was horrified at the practices of the Holy Office, and, in private conversation, criticized its actions. Inevitably, some envious person reported this, and Carlos was arrested. His father made no effort to save him, and he was found guilty of heresy and condemned to death; but, because of his rank, he was permitted to choose the manner of his execution. He elected to have a vein opened, and so bled to death, at the age of 23, in 1568.

In Spanish America, where the Inquisition was not established until 1569, there were fewer condemnations for heresy. As the French writer Frézier remarked, concerning its activities in Chile: 'They busy themselves mainly about the visions of real or pretended sorcerers and certain crimes subject to the Inquisition, like polygamy, etc. For, as for heretics, I am sure they find none, there is so little study there.'

In Mexico, the first victims of the Inquisition were English seamen, members of John Hawkins's expedition of 1567–9, who had been asked to be put ashore after the loss of most of his ships. They had been captured and used as domestic servants; but in 1574 Pedro Moya de Contreras was appointed Inquisitor, and the Englishmen were rounded up and taken to Mexico City. There they were put to the rack:

> And thus having gotten from our own mouths matter sufficient for them to proceed in judgment against us, they caused a large scaffold to be made in the midst of the market-place in Mexico right over against the head church, and 14 or 15 days before the day of their judgment, with the sound of a trumpet and the noise of their *attabalies*, which are a kind of drums, they did assemble the people in all parts of the city; before whom it was then solemnly proclaimed that whosoever would upon such a day repair to the market-place, they should hear the sentence of the Holy Inquisition against the English heretics, Lutherans, and also see the same put in execution. Which being done, and the time approaching of this cruel judgment, the night before they came to the prison where we were with certain officers of that holy hellish house, bringing with them certain fools' coats which they had prepared for us, being called in their language *san benitos*, which coats were made of yellow cotton and red crosses upon them both before and behind …
>
> And so about eight of the clock in the morning we set forth of the prison, every man alone in his yellow coat and a rope about his neck and a

'*we set forth of the prison, every man alone in his yellow coat and a rope about his neck*' great green wax candle in his hand unlighted, having a Spaniard appointed to go upon either side of every one of us. And so, marching in this order and manner towards the scaffold in the market-place, which was a bow-shot distant or thereabouts, we found a great assembly of people all the way, and such a throng that certain of the Inquisitors' officers on horseback were constrained to make way; and so coming to the scaffold we went up by a pair of stairs and found seats ready made and prepared for us to sit down on, every man in order as he should be called to receive his judgment.

We being thus set down as we were appointed, presently the Inquisitors came up another pair of stairs and the Viceroy and all the chief justices with them. When they were set down and placed under the cloth of state agreeing to their degrees and calling, then came up also a great number of friars, White, Black, and Grey, about the number of 300 persons, they being set in the places for them appointed. Then there was a solemn Oyez made and silence commanded, and then presently began their severe and cruel judgment.

The first man that was called was one Roger, the chief armourer of the [ship] *Jesus*, and he had judgment to have 300 stripes on horseback, and after condemned to the galleys as a slave for 10 years.

After him was called John Gray, John Browne, John Rider, John Moon, James Collier, and one Thomas Browne; these were adjudged to have 200 stripes on horseback and after to be committed to the galleys for the space of 8 years. Then was called John Keyes, and was adjudged to have 100 stripes on horseback and condemned to serve in the galleys for the space of 6 years.

Then were severally called the number of

Don Carlos, the eldest son of Philip II. He was found guilty of heresy by the Inquisition, but was allowed to choose the manner of his execution. He bled to death, at the age of 23, in 1568.

53 one after another, and every man had his several judgment, some to have 200 stripes on horseback, and some 100, and condemned for slaves to the galleys, some for 6 years, some for 8, and some for 10. And then was I, Miles Philips, called, and was adjudged to serve in a monastery for 5 years, without any stripes, and to wear a fool's coat or *san benito* during all that time.

Then were called John Story, Richard Williams, David Alexander, Robert Cooke, Paul Horsewell, and Thomas Hull: the six were condemned to serve in monasteries, without stripes, some for three years and some for four … Which being done, and it now drawing toward night, George Rively, Peter Momfry, and Cornelius the Irishman were called and had their judgment to be burnt to ashes, and so were presently sent away to the place of execution in the market-place ... [and] quickly burnt and consumed. And as for us that had received our judgment, being 68 in number, we were carried back that night to prison …

Now after that the time was expired for which we were condemned to serve in those religious houses, we were then brought again before the

Some prisoners at an auto-da-fé *were sentenced to be flogged, or committed to the galleys, but the more obdurate heretics were burned at the conclusion of the ceremony.*

chief Inquisitor and had all our fools' coats pulled off and hanged up in the head church … and every man's name and judgment written thereon with this addition, 'A heretic Lutheran reconciled'. And there were also all their coats hanged up which were condemned to the galleys, and underneath his coat 'Heretic Lutheran reconciled': and also the coats and names of the three that were burned, whereupon was written 'an obstinate heretic Lutheran burnt'.

Altogether, it has been calculated, in 277 years of the Inquisition in Mexico, 41 were burned as relapsed heretics, and 99 burned in effigy. The *auto-da-fé* of 1659 was one of the largest: out of 23 men and six women, seven were burned, five for heresy and two for Judaism; the others were convicted of such varied crimes as blasphemy, bigamy, forgery, perjury, and witchcraft.

others were convicted of such varied crimes as blasphemy, bigamy, forgery, perjury, and witchcraft

In Peru, the Inquisition held 29 *autos-da-fé*, the first in 1581, and the last in 1776. In all, 59 heretics were committed to the stake. In the Portuguese territories of Brazil, the Inquisition was not established, but visiting commissioners were sent there regularly from 1591 onward. Those who were arrested were sent to Lisbon for trial, and no *autos-da-fé* were ever held in Brazil. It has been calculated that between 1591 and 1763 some 400 Jews were shipped to Portugal: 18 were condemned to death, but only one of these, Isaac de Castro, was burned alive (in 1647), the others being garrotted and burned 'in effigy'.

The Inquisition was much more severe in Goa, where more Hindus than Jews were imprisoned. The Portuguese Torres de Castilla described their confinement as:

> … the dirtiest, darkest and most horrible that can possibly be, into which the rays of the sun never penetrate. The kind of noxious air that must be breathed may be imagined when it is known that a dry well in the middle of the space where the prisoners were confined, and which is always uncovered, is used as a privy, the emanations from which have no other outlet for escape than a small opening. The prisoners live in a common privy.

For more than three centuries the Inquisition was active in Spain and Portugal, and their overseas territories. It was suppressed in Spain by Joseph Bonaparte in 1808, restored in 1814, suppressed again in 1820, restored in 1823, and finally suppressed in 1834. Public *autos-da-fé* were banned in Portugal in 1771, and the Inquisition suppressed in 1820. An era of terror, it was hoped, was at an end.

Chapter Six

Torture in England & the Colonies

It is a common fallacy that torture was forbidden by law in England. In fact, its use was proscribed rather by default: English law developed as a combination of common law – what had come to be accepted as the lawful practice – and specific royal statutes; and, since neither of these had ever legalized torture, its use remained outside the law.

In addition, some of the forms of torture described in this book were not recognized as such, but considered rather as legitimate punishment, or as a necessary part of the judicial process of inquiry. The most notorious was the *peine forte et dure*, or 'pressing to plead', which continued in use until the late eighteenth century. When an accused was brought to trial, the law required him to plead 'guilty' or 'not guilty' before the case could be heard. Some persons, however, accused of capital crimes, realizing that if they were found guilty all their property could be seized and their wife and family left destitute, refused to plead.

In his *Survey of London* (1720), John Stow gave this description:

> The criminal is sent back to the prison whence he came, and there laid in some dark room, upon the bare ground on his back, all naked, except his privy parts, his arms and legs drawn with cords fastened to several parts of the room; and then there is laid on his body, iron, stone, or lead, so much as he can bear; the next day he shall have three morsels of barley bread, without drink; and the third day shall have to drink some of the kennel water with bread. And this method is in strictness to be observed until he is dead.

This torture often succeeded in persuading the victim to plead and stand trial. In 1726, for instance, a murderer named Burnworth, arraigned at Kingston assizes, endured a mass of some 204kg (450lb) for nearly two hours before he begged to be released; he pleaded, was found guilty, and hanged.

(Opposite) The treatment of slaves in the British colonies was brutal. Many were branded with a red-hot iron to denote their ownership, and sadistic flogging was a common occurrence.

The peine forte et dure: *a brutal aspect of the English judicial system that continued for more than four centuries. Those who refused to plead 'guilty' or 'not guilty' were sentenced to be pressed to death.*

However, the *peine forte et dure* was in fact designed as the punishment itself. As originally defined in a statute of Edward I in 1275, it was to be 'strong and hard prison'; but in 1406 pressing to death under weights became the sentence. A typical case is that of Walter Calverley, a Yorkshireman who was pressed to death at York Castle two centuries later on 10 August 1605:

In an insane moment ... he killed his two sons ... attempted to kill his wife ... and rode off to murder his boy Henry, who was placed out to be nursed, but being overtaken and captured, he was examined before Sir John Savile and Sir Thomas Bland, on the 24th of April 1605 (the same day as the funeral of the boys, and the day after the murders) who sent him temporarily to Wakefield.

Soon afterwards he was conveyed to York Castle, where he was found guilty and sentenced to death ... Having come to his senses he refused to plead (and in so doing proved his return to sanity) in order to save his goods and estate for his only remaining son, Henry, who lived to enjoy them. He was therefore called to endure the *peine forte et dure*, that is, being pressed to death.

J. Horsfall Turner,
Wakefield House of Correction (1904)

Luke Owen Pike, in *A History of Crime in England* (1873), stated that it was usual to hasten death by placing a sharp piece of timber under the victim's back, but this was not always permitted. In February 1658, Major George Strangeways, a distinguished soldier of the Civil War, refused to plead to a charge of murder:

He was prohibited that usuall Favour in that kind, to have a piece of Timber layed under his back to Accelerate its penetration, and the Assistants laid on a first weight, which finding it too light for a sudden Execution, many of those standing by added their own weight to disburthen him of his pain. In the space of eight or ten minutes at the most, his unfettered Soul left her tortur'd Mansion. ...

A terrible case occurred as late as 1735, at Nottingham assizes, when an alleged murderer, apparently deaf and dumb from birth, was unable to plead, and was pressed to death. The judges believed that the accused had only pretended to be dumb, as was discovered – too late for the prisoner to plead – to be the case in Ireland in 1740.

Mathew Ryan was accused of highway robbery at Kilkenny assizes. A moving description of the incident was published in *The Percy Anecdotes* (vol VIII, 1823):

> The judges on this desired the prisoner to plead, but he still pretended to be insensible to all that was said to him. The law now called for the *peine forte et dure*; but the judges compassionately deferred awarding it until a future day, in the hope that he might in the meantime acquire a juster sense of his situation. When again brought up, however, the criminal persisted in his refusal to plead: and the court at last pronounced the dreadful sentence, that he should be pressed to death. The sentence was accordingly executed upon him two days after in the public market-place of Kilkenny. As the weights were heaping on the wretched man, he earnestly supplicated to be hanged; but it being beyond the power of the sheriff to deviate from the mode of punishment prescribed in the sentence, even this was an indulgence which could no longer be granted to him.

By order of the Council

The use of other instruments of torture, particularly the rack, was not permissible under common law, nor was it named in any statute, and so a special licence had to be obtained from the Crown. Generally this was made by an order in Privy Council, or later by the notorious Star Chamber; for example, in 1310 a royal warrant was issued to authorize the torture of the arrested Templars (see Chapter 3, page 49). Moreover, the Treason Act of 1351 made it almost certain that royal permission would be obtained for the torture of anyone suspected of conspiracy against the king. In 1468, during the Wars of the Roses, the Lord Mayor of London, Sir Thomas Coke, was found guilty of treason on the evidence of a single witness that he had confessed on the rack. It is believed that the rack was introduced into England around 1420 by

an alleged murderer, apparently deaf and dumb from birth, was unable to plead

*'he was this day
racked before
torture, in torture,
between torture,
and after torture'*

the Duke of Exeter, who was Constable of the Tower of London at the time; its victims were described as being 'married to the Duke of Exeter's daughter'.

The Star Chamber was named after a room in the Palace of Westminster, the ceiling of which was painted with stars. Originally, this was the meeting place of the king's council, which heard appeals and dealt with matters outside the jurisdiction of the ordinary courts. However, soon after the accession of Henry VIII in 1509, his chancellor Thomas (later Cardinal) Wolsey began to use the Court of Star Chamber as his own instrument of justice, and his secretary and successor, Thomas Cromwell, consolidated the court's wide-ranging powers. Comprising two senior justices and members of the Privy Council, the Star Chamber was at its most active during the reign of Elizabeth I. It became increasingly arbitrary in its decisions, and was the principal instigator of torture, but continued until a flooding tide of protest brought about its abolition in the reign of Charles I in 1640.

Many documents of the time are evidence of the acceptance of torture by the Privy Council; in particular the use of the rack. For instance:

> On the 9th June 1555, letters were written to the Lord North and others [that is, by order of Queen Elizabeth to the Privy Council], to put such obstinate persons as would not confess to the torture, and there to order them at their discretion; and a letter was written to the lieutenant of the Tower to the same effect.
>
> On 28 December 1566, a letter was addressed by the Privy Council to the Attorney-General and others, that: where they were heretofore appointed to put Clement Fisher, now prisoner in the Tower, in some fear of torture. Whereby his lewdness and such as he might detect might the better come to light, they are requested, for that the said Fisher is not minded to feel some touch of the rack.

Fearful of Spanish plots to assassinate her, suspicious of anybody who might claim a right – however distant – to the succession to the throne, and desperate to establish the Church of England as independent of any influence from Rome, Elizabeth could easily be persuaded that treason was in the air. Not only Jesuit priests, smuggled into the country, apprehended, and accused of being Spanish spies, went in fear of the rack. Edward Peacham, the rector of Hinton St George in Somerset, preached a sermon that was considered treasonable: he was carried to the Tower, where the lieutenant reported: 'he was this day racked before torture, in torture, between torture, and after torture'. Even common

robbers were 'to be brought to the rack and to feel the smart there, if the examiners by their discretion shall think good, for the better boulting out of the truth of the matter'.

In 1571, the queen signed a warrant to Sir Thomas Smith and Dr Wilson, authorizing two of the Duke of Norfolk's servants, Bannister and Barker, 'to be put to the rack and find the taste thereof'. The duke was on trial for intriguing with Mary Stuart, the captive queen of Scotland, who had a legitimate claim to the throne of England. Sir Thomas Smith reported:

A victim being 'married to the Duke of Exeter's daughter', the rack. It was reputed to have been introduced to England by the Duke of Exeter, who was Constable of the Tower, around 1420.

I suppose we have gotten so mych at this time as is lyke to be had; yet tomorrow we do intend to bryng a couple of them to the rack, not in any hope to get any thyng worthy that payne or feare, but because it is earnestly commanded unto us.

Subsequently, he announced 'of Bannister with the rack, and Barker with the extreme fear of it, we suppose we have gotten all'.

The official rackmaster of the time was Thomas Norton, who boasted that he had stretched the Jesuit Alexander Briant 'one good foot longer than ever God made him'. On 27 March 1582, he wrote to the Secretary of State, Sir Thomas Walsingham:

> None was put to the rack that was not at first by some manifest evidence known to the Council to be guilty of treason, so that it was well assured beforehand that there was no innocent tormented. Also none was tormented to know whether he was guilty or not, but for the Queen's safety to know the manner of the treason and the accomplices.

The Privy Council, in fact, was employing torture for much the same reasons and in the same way as the Inquisition. And the assurances of Lord Burghley (the queen's chief minister and Lord High Treasurer) in 1583 strikingly echo the writings of the Inquisition's jurists:

> The Queen's servants, the warders [of the Tower], whose office and act it is to handle the rack, were ever by those that attended the examinations, specially charged to use it in as charitable manner as such a thing might be.

A form of torture used in the prison at Ely, Cambridgeshire. The prisoner was laid across a series of iron bars, and chained in place. An iron collar, weighing some 3kg (over 7lb) and fitted with spikes 30cm (1ft) long, prevented him from resting his head. A heavy iron bar was then placed across his legs, and fastened to one of them, so that he was unable to move.

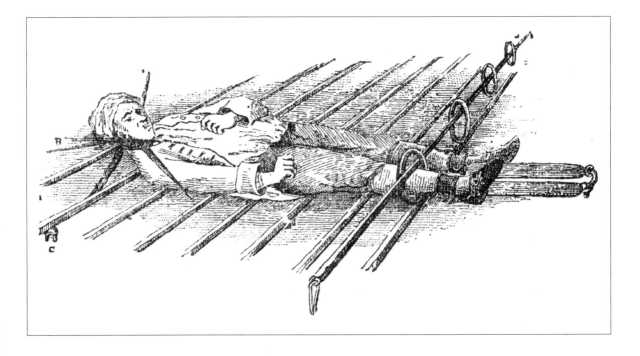

But those who suffered the rack would hardly imagine their torturers to be charitable. One of these was Francis Throckmorton, a Catholic who was involved in a plot for the invasion of England and the release of Mary Stuart in 1583. In his *History of England*, the historian J.A. Froude imagined the scene in the Tower of London:

> Interrogated in the gloomy cell which had rung with the screams of the Jesuits, the horrid instrument at his side, with the mute executioners standing ready to strain his limbs out of their sockets, his imagination was appalled, his senses refused to do their work. He equivocated, varied in his story, contradicted himself in every succeeding sentence. Pardon was promised him if he would make a free confession. He still held out, but he could not conceal that he had much to tell, and the times did not permit humanity to traitors to imperil the safety of the realm.
>
> The Queen gave the necessary authority to proceed with 'the pains'. Her Majesty thought it agreeable with good policy and the safety of her person and throne, to commit to the hands of her learned council, to assay by torture to draw the truth from him. Again he was proffered pardon; again he refused, and he was handed over 'to such as were usually appointed in the Tower to handle the rack'. His honour struggled with his agony. On the first racking he confessed nothing; but he could not endure a second trial. ... Sitting in wretchedness beside the horrid engine, the November light faintly streaming down the tunnelled windows, he broke his pledged word, and broke his heart along with it.

His guilt confirmed out of his own mouth, Throckmorton was drawn on a hurdle to Tyburn, hanged, drawn, and quartered, on 10 July 1584.

In Scotland, torture was even more widely used than in England, particularly during the seventeenth-century trials of witches (see Chapter 7, pages 118–21). So, when Guy Fawkes and his fellow-conspirators were arrested after the failure of their plot to blow up Parliament, the new king, James VI of Scotland and I of England, did not hesitate to insist upon torture. In a letter that he signed on 6 November 1605 he specified for 'such a desperate fellow' as Fawkes that 'the gentler Tortures are to be first used upon him *et sic per gradus ad ima tenditur*' – and so by degrees moving to the worst – 'and so God spede your good work.'

These 'gentler tortures' were no doubt the manacles, which had been widely used during Elizabeth's reign. Standing on a stool, the accused was hung by the wrists against a wall, wearing iron gauntlets that could be gradually tightened as necessary; the stool was then removed,

'Sitting in wretchedness beside the horrid engine, he broke his pledged word, and his heart also'

After enduring agonies on the rack, those found guilty of treason were publicly beheaded. Then it was the duty of the executioner to hold up the head, crying: 'Behold the head of a traitor! So die all traitors!'

and the accused left dangling for many hours. The sadistic Richard Topcliffe, who tortured the Jesuit Father Edmund Campion more than ten times, remarked: 'It will be as though he were dancing a trick or figure'. When Campion was tried in Westminster Hall in 1581, he was incapable of lifting his hand to plead, and two of his fellow priests had to raise it for him.

Historians dispute whether Guy Fawkes endured the manacles and the rack. According to Father John Gerard – one of only a few Jesuit priests who survived Topcliffe's attentions, and who eventually escaped to the Continent – 'the common voice was that he was extremely racked in the first few days'; but Sir Edward Hoby, a member of the king's household, wrote that only the manacles had been used. What is sure is that by 8 November Fawkes was beginning to talk, revealing details of the plot, and giving names. All the other conspirators, who had fled away from London, were rounded up, and four were killed while resisting arrest. Fawkes was interrogated for three days, and signed a confession each night. His signatures, deteriorating steadily to a mere scrawl, give an indication of his physical state, and are mute evidence of the tortures he had suffered.

Those arrested included not only the conspirators, but also the priests who had attended them. Lord Salisbury, the king's chief minister, recommended that 'the prisoners should be confined apart, in darkness, and examined by torchlight, and that the tortures be slow and at intervals, as being most effectual'; and three weeks later he protested at the conspirators' refusals to incriminate the priests, 'yea, whatsoever torture they are put to'.

The trial of the eight surviving conspirators began in Westminster Hall on 27 January 1606. The outcome was inevitable, and they were hanged, drawn, and quartered three days later. But there were still more prisoners, and orders for their torture were issued by the Privy Council on 19 February.

The most important of these 'inferior sort' was Nicholas Owen, otherwise known as Little John, a carpenter who had constructed countless 'priests' holes' in the houses of Catholics. He was very small, with a crippled leg and a hernia, and by law – and common decency – should have been exempted from torture by his condition; but he had valuable information about the hiding places in which priests might be discovered. He was subjected to the manacles, and his suffering was such that his belly had to be held in place by an iron plate. Although he confessed to having known the conspirators – a matter of no importance, since they were already dead – he steadfastly refused to give up a single detail of his priests' holes, and died in great agony early in the morning of 2 March. The government claimed that Owen had committed suicide by ripping open his belly with a knife supplied with his food, but his prison keeper told a relative that following the torture his hands were so crippled that he could not even feed himself.

The principal conspirators in the plot to assassinate King James on 5 November 1605. Fawkes was tortured for three days before he confessed. Historians disagree on whether or not he was racked, but he certainly suffered the manacles. The deterioration in the condition of his hands is evident from the changes in his signature (above).

The final torture

The ultimate torment, slow death by burning at the stake, was practised in England and Scotland for several centuries, not only for heresy or witchcraft, but for the 'petty treason' of murdering a husband. Sometimes a degree of mercy was allowed: the victim was strangled as the flames took hold. In Lincoln in 1722, Eleanor Elsom was convicted of killing her husband, and sentenced to be burned. Her clothes and limbs were smeared with pitch, and she was dragged on a hurdle to the place of execution. She was made to stand on a barrel of pitch surrounded by faggots, and chained to the stake. A noose was placed about her neck, the rope running through a pulley at the top of the stake and into the executioner's hands. The fire was lit, and the rope was pulled; but whether Eleanor was dead before the flames finally consumed her body half an hour later, nobody knew.

Sometimes, the use of the rope obviously failed. Joseph Strutt, in his *Manners and Customs of the Inhabitants of England* (1775), described the execution of Catherine Hayes at Tyburn in 1726:

The letter of the law to this very day, I believe, condemns a woman, who doth murder her husband, to be burnt alive … In the case of Catherine Hayes (who, for the murder of her husband, some few years ago, was adjudged to suffer death at the stake), the intention was first to strangle her; but as they used at that time to draw a rope which was fastened round the culprit's neck, and came through a staple of the stake, but at the very moment that the fire was put to the wood which was set around, the flames sometimes reached the offenders before they were quite strangled – just so it happened to her; for the fire taking quick hold of the wood, and the wind being brisk, blew the smoke and blaze so full in the faces of the executioners, who were pulling at the rope, that they were obliged to let go their hold before they had quite strangled her; so that, as I have been informed by some there present, she suffered much torment before she died. But now they are first hanged at the stake until they are quite dead, and then the fire is kindled round, and the body burnt to ashes.

The last woman to die in this way was Christian Murphy, alias Bowman, found guilty of coining, who was burned in March 1789. A year later the law was changed, women being condemned to hanging for their crimes.

Other victims were allowed to have small bags of gunpowder hung round their necks and waists, but even this was not always effective. Henry Moore's *Complete Protestant Martyrology* (1809) gives a horribly detailed account of the death of Dr John Hooper, Lord Bishop of Gloucester, who was burned for heresy during the reign of the Catholic Mary I in 1555:

Other victims were allowed to have small bags of gunpowder hung round their necks

Being now in his shirt, he trussed it between his legs, where he had a pound of gunpowder in a bladder, and under each arm the same quantity. He now went up to the stake, where three iron hoops were brought … The iron hoop was then put round his waist, which being made too short, he shrank and put in his belly with his hand; but when they offered to bind his neck and legs he refused them, saying, 'I am well assured I shall not trouble you' … Then the reeds were thrown up, and he received two bundles of them in his own hands, and put one under each arm.

Command was now given that the fire should be kindled; but, owing to the number of green faggots, it was some time before the flames set fire to the reeds. The wind being adverse, and the morning very cold, the flames blew from him, so that he was scarcely touched by the fire. Another fire was soon kindled of a more vehement nature: it was now the bladders of gunpowder exploded, but they proved of no service to the suffering prelate. He now prayed with a loud voice, 'Lord Jesus, have mercy upon me; Lord Jesus, have mercy upon me; Lord Jesus, receive my spirit': and these were the last words he was heard to utter.

But even when his face was completely black with the flames, and his tongue swelled so that he could not speak, yet his lips went till they were shrunk to the gums; and he knocked his breast with his hands until one of his arms fell off, and then continued knocking with the other while the fat, water, and blood dripped out at his finger ends. At length, by renewing of the fire, his strength was gone, and his hand fastened in the iron which was put round him. Soon after, the whole lower part of his body being consumed, he fell over the iron that bound him, into the fire … This holy martyr was more than *three quarters of an hour* consuming, the inexpressible anguish of which he endured … moving neither forwards, backwards, nor to any side: his nether parts were consumed, and his bowels fell out some time before he expired.

Flogging in the army and navy

Once Britain had finally established a standing army in the late seventeenth century, the maintenance of discipline among the soldiery became a necessity. The Mutiny Act of 1689 authorized that flogging with the cat-o'-nine-tails should be the standard method of punishment in the army.

The sensation was said to be 'as though the talons of a hawk were tearing the flesh off the bones'.

The 'cat' was made up of nine separate lengths of whipcord, each being tied with three knots at separate places along its length. The victim was strapped to a wooden triangle and beaten, often by the regimental drummer. The thin cords would slash through the victim's skin at each stroke, while the knots tore out gobbets of flesh. The sensation was said to be 'as though the talons of a hawk were tearing the flesh off the bones'.

Throughout the eighteenth century, floggings could be ordered for quite trivial offences: one soldier at Gibraltar, sentenced for being dirty on parade, was beaten so severely that he died a few days later. A court martial had the power to order as many as 1000 lashes, and sentences of 500 to 800 were common. This form of punishment continued into the nineteenth century, as was reported by *Tait's Edinburgh Magazine* in 1833:

A soldier of the First Regiment of Grenadier Guards, of which the Duke of Wellington is Colonel, having been convicted of insubordination, intoxication on duty, and of refusal to deliver up his arms when ordered by his officer, was sentenced to receive 500 lashes. After receiving 200 lashes, the surgeon of the regiment interfered, and put a stop to the brutal punishment, in consequence of the life of the soldier being in danger. The soldier was then removed to the military hospital in a hackney coach, his back being dreadfully lacerated. As a sort of refinement in cruelty, and to increase the severity of a punishment which could not be inflicted to the full extent without depriving the unfortunate culprit of his life, a fresh hand was procured at every 20 lashes.

In some regiments, the interval between each stroke of the cat was determined by the tapping of a drum, the rate of taps having been instructed to the drummer beforehand. The longer the interval, the greater the pain the victim suffered. Many were not as fortunate as the soldier in the report above. For example, if he was judged incapable of receiving the full 500 lashes at one time, a soldier might be returned to his cell until his wounds were partially healed, when he would be brought back to receive the rest of his sentence. When the sentence was 800 or 1000 lashes, the full punishment was often spread over three or four separate occasions.

A soldier who was flogged in 1832 described what he suffered:

I felt an astounding sensation between the shoulders under my neck, which went to my toe-nails in one direction, and my finger-nails in another, and stung me to the heart, as if a knife had gone through my body … He came on a second time a few inches lower, and then I thought the former stroke was sweet and agreeable compared with that one … I felt my flesh quiver in every nerve, from the scalp of my head to my toe-nails. The time between each stroke seemed so long as to be agonizing, and yet the next came too soon. The pain in my lungs was more severe, I thought, than on my back. I felt as if I would burst in the internal parts of my body …

I put my tongue between my teeth, held it there, and bit it almost in two pieces. What with the blood from my tongue, and my lips, which I had also bitten, and the blood from my lungs, or some other internal part, ruptured by the writhing agony, I was almost choked, and became black in the face … Only fifty had been inflicted, and the time since they began was like a long period of life; I felt as if I had lived all the time of my real life in pain and torture, and that the time when existence had pleasure in it was a dream, long, long gone by.

A British soldier being flogged for a minor offence. The strokes of the 'cat' were timed by the drummer's beats on his drum. The slower the beat, the more intense the pain of the punishment.

The Royal Navy was also not established until the seventeenth century, but the practice of flogging aboard royal fighting ships or armed privateers was of long standing. The naval 'cat' was made from a piece of rope, about 1.5m (5ft) in length, and as thick as a man's wrist. The last 0.5m (20ins) was separated into strands, each twisted tightly, and knotted at several points along its length. The offender was tied to one of the gratings that covered the hatches, which was secured against the ship's side. A nineteenth-century writer reported:

Flogging in the Royal Navy in the 18th century. The offender was tied to one of the gratings that covered the ship's hatches, and lashed with a 'cat' of rope about 1.5m (5ft) in length. The last third of the rope was separated into strands, twisted and knotted.

In the Army, the drummer who flogs stands on one spot, and delivers the lash without moving his position, his arm alone giving force to the blow: but in the Navy, the boatswain's mate, who has this duty to perform, stands full two strides from the delinquent; he 'combs out the cat', as it is termed, by running his fingers through the strands, and separating them from each other, after every lash; then waving it over his head, he takes a step forward, and, with an inflexion of his body that gives his whole strength to the operation, delivers the stroke at the full sweep of his arm. 'Tis a severe punishment thus; and I do not think any man could stand nine dozen as I have seen it 'laid in'. An unhallowed torture it is – bad as the rack of bygone times; and to the man that deserved such a punishment, hanging would be a more merciful dispensation.

Torture in the colonies

When the first English colonies were established in America during the early seventeenth century, they came at first under the general provisions of common and statute law; but the Privy Council and Star Chamber were over the other side of the Atlantic, and there is no evidence that the rack or similar instruments of torture were ever used. No witch was ever burned in New England, but slaves who murdered their masters – an act of treason – were burned alive.

The most notorious use of torture of free citizens occurred in the trials of those accused of witchcraft at Salem in 1692. The penalty of the *peine forte et dure* had been abolished in Massachusetts by the 1641 Body of Liberties – 'For bodily punishments we allow amongst us none that are inhumane, barbarous or cruel' – but it was nevertheless imposed upon 80-year-old Giles Cory, who refused to plead. He died slowly over a period of two days, and 'in pressing, his tongue being pressed out of his mouth, the sheriff with his cane forced it in again'.

Confessions of witchcraft were obtained by torture of a crude sort:

> Here are five persons who have lately confessed themselves to be witches and do accuse some of us of being along with them … Two of the five are [Martha] Carrier's sons, young men who would not confess anything till they tied them neck and heels till the blood was ready to come out of their noses. And 'tis credibly believed and reported this was the occasion of making them confess that they never did …
> Quoted in Robert Calef, *More Wonders of the Invisible World* (1700)

Apart from Giles Cory, 19 of the accused, including the Rev George Burroughs, were hanged, and two more died in jail.

The judicial use of torture was at this time rare in the colonies. On the other hand, violent and sadistic practices in the name of discipline by private individuals were scarcely frowned on. African slaves – as well as convicted criminals from England who were transported and committed to slavery – were regularly flogged, even for minor misdemeanours, until well into the nineteenth century. Women were the victims as often as men. In Jamaica, in 1829, the Rev G.W. Bridges was accused of the ill-treatment of a young girl: he had stripped her, hung her by her hands from a hook in the ceiling, and flogged her until she was 'a mass of lacerated flesh and gore'. He was acquitted at his hearing. In 1830, also in Jamaica, a servant, Eleanor Mead, was beaten. According to the *Anti-Slavery Monthly Reporter* (1829):

> Her mistress, Mrs Earnshaw … a lady of humanity and delicacy, having taken offence at something this slave had said or done … ordered her to be stripped naked, prostrated on the ground, and in her own presence caused the male driver to inflict upon her bared body 58 lashes of the cart-whip … When one hip had been sufficiently lacerated in the opinion of Mrs Earnshaw, she told the driver to go round and flog the other side.

But this was nothing compared with the work of a planter named Huggins, who submitted 'twenty-one of his slaves, men and women,

'they tied them neck and heels till the blood was ready to come out of their noses'

to upwards of three thousand lashes of the cart-whip' in the market-place of Nevis. One woman alone was struck 291 times, and one man received a total of 365 lashes.

The Jamaican cart-whip was indeed a fearsome instrument of pain. It was between 3.5 and 4.5m (12 to 15ft) long, tapering from a breadth of over 5cm (2ins) at the handle – itself 0.5m (20ins) long – to the thickness of a cord at the tip. In a speech delivered to the island Assembly in 1826, one of the representatives declared: 'I do say that 39 lashes with this horrid instrument can be made more grievous than 500 lashes with the "cat".'

However, the use of the cart-whip was legal. An Act passed by the legislature in Jamaica – also in 1826 – made it an offence for any slave-driver to administer more than 10 lashes at any one time (for any one offence), or for any owner, overseer or jailer to administer more than 39.

It was also quite common for the victim to be flogged soundly with a tamarind switch, after the 39 lashes with a cart-whip – indeed, it was

As in Greek and Roman times, slaves had no standing or rights in the British colonies, well into the 19th century. They were regularly flogged by their owners – and not always as a punishment. Many planters derived sadistic pleasure from seeing their slaves beaten, or even inflicting the lashing themselves.

claimed that this would 'beat out the bruised blood'. The switch was a thin cane, made of the wood of the tamarind tree; it was very flexible, and as hard as wire. Beatings were also carried out with switches made from the thorny branches of the ebony plant.

In the jails, slaves were 'bowsed' (a naval term meaning to stretch out with block and tackle) for flogging. An account in the *Jamaica Christian Record* for 1830 provides the distasteful details:

> A female ... about 22 years of age, was then laid down, with her face downwards; her wrists were secured by cords run into nooses; her ankles were brought together and placed in another noose; the cord composing this last one, passed through a block, connected with a post. The cord was tightened, and the young woman was then stretched to her utmost length.
>
> A female then advanced, and raised her clothes towards her head, leaving the person indecently exposed. The boatswain of the workhouse, a tall athletic man, flourished his whip four or five times round his head, and proceeded with the punishment. This instrument of punishment was a cat, formed of knotted cords. The blood sprang from the wounds it inflicted. The poor creature shrieked in agony ...

The treatment of slaves in the United States was no better. Harriet Beecher Stowe, the author of *Uncle Tom's Cabin* (1852), quoted a description of punishment in the prison of New Orleans:

> Entering a large paved courtyard, around which ran galleries filled with slaves of all ages, sexes, and colours, I heard the snap of a whip, every stroke of which sounded like the sharp crack of a pistol. I turned my head, and beheld a sight which absolutely chilled me to the marrow of my bones, and gave me, for the first time in my life, the sensation of my hair stiffening at the roots.
>
> There lay a black girl flat upon her face, on a board, her two thumbs tied, and fastened to one end, her feet tied and drawn tightly to the other end, while a strap passed over the small of her back, and, fastened around the board, compressed her closely to it. Below the strap she was entirely naked.
>
> By her side, and six feet [two metres] off, stood a huge negro, with a long whip, which he applied with dreadful power and wonderful precision. Every stroke brought away a strip of skin, which clung to the lash, or fell quivering on the pavement, while the blood followed after it. The poor creature writhed and shrieked, and, in a voice which

'There lay a naked black girl flat upon her face, on a board'

showed alike her fear of death and her dreadful agony, screamed to her master, who stood at her head, 'Oh, spare my life! don't cut my soul out!'. But still fell the horrid lash; still strip after strip peeled off from the skin; gash after gash was cut in her living flesh, until it became a livid and bloody mass of raw and quivering muscle.

The native inhabitants of the West Indies suffered as much, if not more, at the hands both of the original Spanish settlers, and the British who followed them. In *The History of the British Colonies in the West Indies* (1793), Bryan Edwards quotes an eyewitness account:

> I once beheld four or five principal Indians roasted alive at a slow fire, and as the miserable victims poured forth dreadful screams, which disturbed the commanding officer in his afternoon slumbers, he sent word that they should be strangled, but the officer on guard …would not suffer it; but causing their mouths to be gagged, that their cries might not be heard, he stirred up the fire with his own hands, and roasted them deliberately till they all expired …

'they soon after hung him up by the testicles, giving him infinite blows'

It was a violent age, and the early American settlers committed acts of cruelty that the law, or their consciences, might well have prevented in Europe. When Sir Henry Morgan and his buccaneers captured the Spanish city of Panama in 1671, they took a large quantity of prisoners, as described in John Esquemeling's *Buccaneers of America* (1684):

> One poor and miserable wretch was found in the house of a gentleman of great quality, who had put on … a pair of taffety breeches belonging to his master with a little silver key hanging at the strings thereof. This being perceived by the Pirates, they immediately asked him where was the cabinet of the said key. His answer was: He knew not what was become of it, but only that, finding those breeches in his master's house, he had made bold to wear them. Not being able to extort any other confession out of him, they first put him upon the rack, wherewith they inhumanly disjointed his arms. After this, they twisted a cord about his forehead, which they wrung so hard that his eyes appeared as big as eggs and were ready to fall out of his skull. But neither with these torments could they obtain any positive answer to their demands. Whereupon they soon after hung him up by the testicles, giving him infinite blows and stripes while he was under that intolerable pain and posture of body. Afterwards they cut off his nose and ears, and singed his face with burning straw, till he could speak nor lament his misery no longer.

Then, losing all hopes of hearing any confession from this mouth, they commanded a negro to run him through with a lance, which put an end to his life and a period to their cruel and inhuman tortures.

No doubt many other acts of equal brutality took place on the American continent, in the battle for possession of the New World. But the Age of Enlightenment was dawning, and in England, and elsewhere in Europe, there were movements afoot to bring torture to an end.

The buccaneers of Henry Morgan's band tortured many of their prisoners when they invaded Panama in 1671.

Chapter Seven

European Witch-Hunts

During the twentieth century, sweeping claims have been made that witchcraft survived through several thousand years as a tradition of an ancient religion: the worship of the Mother Goddess. There is little evidence for this, nor is there reason to suppose that the witchcraft practised in much of medieval Europe was anything other than primitive folk superstition, combined with a smattering of herbal lore. The 'wise woman' who could 'charm' away warts, make a barren wife fertile, or ease the pains of childbirth, was a valued member of the peasant community – even if she was feared for her 'supernatural powers'.

But, about the time of the millennium, there had been more sinister developments. In the eleventh century, there was a sudden growth in all kinds of religious activity. Although many scholars deny the suggestion, it is tempting to think that this was due (at least in part) to the disappointment that 1000 years had come and gone without the expected end of the world, the Second Coming, the raising of the dead, and the Last Judgment. Perhaps God was dissatisfied with the piety of his people, and had turned his face from them.

This era saw the Roman Catholic Church attempt to strengthen the faith, through the establishment of the major monastic orders, the building of great cathedrals, the encouragement of pilgrimages, and the crusades against the infidel. However, in the countryside, far from the city cathedrals and the monasteries, some people turned against the Church. They had little to draw on but the Christian beliefs that they and their forebears had been raised in; and so they perhaps wondered whether God's great adversary, the Devil, was more likely to protect them. On the other hand, they may only have returned to the practice of pagan rituals that had survived in a primitive form for centuries.

One thousand years later we cannot know exactly what took place. The only early accounts are by churchmen who naturally felt threatened by anything that questioned established beliefs, and who undoubtedly exaggerated and sensationalized their reports. There were witches, it was said, who met together at feasts, or sabbats, and who could fly through the air and change their shape into animals or other beings. For

(Opposite) Matthew Hopkins, the self-appointed 'Witch Finder General', sought out witchcraft in East Anglia in the years 1645 and 1646. Forced to give up the 'swimming' of witches, he resorted principally to dis-orientation techniques, keeping his victims awake for days at a time, until they would confess to anything.

several centuries, theologians argued that these abilities were illusions or fantasies, that witches had only dreamt or imagined them – possibly under the influence of their herbal potions.

Nevertheless, if the witches themselves believed in their abilities, they were as guilty of heresy as if they truly possessed them. This dictum was first formulated in a document known as the *Canon Episcopi*, which was published in the tenth century, and made part of canon law in the twelfth century. It begins:

> Bishops and their officials must labour with all their strength to uproot thoroughly from their parishes the pernicious art of sorcery and malefice invented by the Devil, and if they find a man or woman follower of this wickedness to eject them foully disgraced from their parishes …

'without question the most important and most sinister work on demonology ever written'

There is no mention here of any form of punishment other than the implied one of excommunication, a natural outcome of heretical practices. Such heresy might be the Devil's invention, but at this point there was no explicit suggestion that it involved his worship. It was not until the thirteenth century that the popes began to take a serious interest in witchcraft, and it was 1484 when Innocent VIII published the bull that launched the great witch-hunts of the sixteenth and seventeenth centuries. Known as *Summis desiderantes affectibus* ('desiring with the most profound anxiety'), it states:

> It has recently come to our attention … that in some parts of northern Germany … many persons … have abused themselves with devils, incubi and succubi, and by their incantations, spells, conjurations, and other accursed superstitions and horrid charms, … destroy the offspring of women and the young of cattle, blast and eradicate the produce of the earth, the grapes of the vine, and the fruits of trees … Furthermore, these wretches afflict and torment men and women, beasts of burden, herd beasts, as well as cattle of other kinds, with pain and disease, both internal and external; they hinder men from generating and women from conceiving … Above and beyond this, they blasphemously renounce the Faith that they received by the Sacrament of Baptism, and at the instigation of the Enemy of the human race they do not shrink from committing and perpetrating the foulest abominations and excesses to the peril of their souls, whereby they offend the Divine Majesty and are a cause of scandal and dangerous example to very many …
>
> Wherefore We, as is our duty, desirous of removing all hindrances and obstacles whatsoever by which the work of the Inquisitors may be

impeded, as also to apply potent remedies to prevent the disease of heresy and other turpitudes diffusing their poison to the destruction of other innocent souls ... decree and enjoin that the aforesaid Inquisitors be empowered to proceed to the correction, imprisonment and punishment of any persons for the said abominations and enormities ...

The 'aforesaid Inquisitors', who had in fact drafted the bull for Innocent's signature, were two Dominican professors of theology, Heinrich Kramer and Jacob Sprenger. Taking advantage of the new invention of printing, they included the text of the bull in their handbook for witch-hunters, *Malleus Maleficarum* (*Hammer of the Witches*), which was published in 1486, and which has been described by Rossell Hope Robbins, in his *Encyclopedia of Witchcraft & Demonology*, as:

... without question the most important and most sinister work on demonology ever written. It crystallized into a fiercely stringent code combining previous folklore about black magic with church dogma on heresy and, if any one work could, opened the floodgates of the inquisitorial hysteria. It sought to make effective the biblical command of Exodus xxii.18: 'Thou shalt not suffer a witch to live'.

The book, which was republished in at least 13 editions up to 1520, and reprinted in another 16 between 1574 and 1669, was designed to provide detailed guidance for the civil authorities, so that they could

A handbook for witch-hunters, The Malleus Maleficarum, was first published in 1486, and reprinted many times over the next two centuries.

When the North Berwick witches
(see pages 118–19)
were brought before the king, James VI (later James I of England), who personally interrogated them in the palace of Holyrood.

take over the inquisition of witches from the religious courts, and go directly to the sentencing and execution of the condemned. It is divided into three parts. The first discusses the necessity for inquisitors thoroughly to understand the enormity of the heresy of witchcraft; and the second describes the doings of witches, how they may be detected, and how they may be countered. It is the third part that was to have such a horrific influence. It was probably written by Kramer, who had considerable practical experience of the subject, and it provides the rules for taking legal action against witches and securing their conviction. It describes the examination of witnesses, and the arrest, imprisonment, questioning, and the torture of the accused.

Torture was necessary because it was generally accepted that a witch could not be condemned without her (or his) own confession of guilt. And a voluntary confession was considered insufficient: only a confession obtained through pain and torment could be assumed to come truly from the heart. As one writer pointed out, many convicted witches were regular attendants in church, and no one would have suspected them of witchcraft if they had not been tortured, when they confessed to all sorts of sinful practices.

Few churchmen perceived that the logic of this argument was inherently false: that the torture would invariably be continued until a confession was obtained. One poor woman, shortly before her execution, told her minister that her confession, and her denunciations of others named as accomplices, were false. He begged her to recant and – even if she could not save herself – redeem the lives of the innocent. But she replied:

Look, Father, look at my legs: they are like fire – ready to burn up – so excruciating is the pain. I could not bear to have so much as a fly touch them, to say nothing of submitting once more to torture. I would a hundred times rather die than endure such frightful agony again. I cannot describe to anybody how terrible the pain actually is.

The torture was designed to be carried out in several stages, each one increasingly painful. In the *Malleus Maleficarum* Kramer gives detailed instructions on the first stage, the 'preparatory question':

First, the gaolers prepare the implements, then they strip the prisoner (if it be a woman, she has already been stripped by other women, upright and of good repute). This stripping is lest some means of witchcraft may have been sewn into the clothing – such as often, taught by the Devil, they prepare from the bodies of unbaptized infants, that they may forfeit salvation.

And when the implements of torture have been prepared, the judge, both in person and through other good men, zealous in the faith, tries to persuade the prisoner to confess the truth freely; but, if he will not confess, he bids the attendants prepare the prisoner for the strappado or other torture. The attendants obey forthwith, yet with feigned agitation. Then, at the prayer of some of those present, the prisoner is loosed again, and is taken aside and once more begged to confess, being led to believe that he will in that case not be put to death …

But if, neither by threats nor by promises such as these, the witch cannot be induced to speak the truth, then the gaolers must carry out the sentence, and torture the prisoner according to the accepted methods, with more or less severity as the delinquent's crime may demand.

However, the law allowed torture to be repeated only if new, unconfessed indications of guilt were expected, and so this preliminary stage was often considered not to be torture at all. Many court records contain the phrase 'the prisoner confessed without torture'. In any case, the lawyers came up with the excuse that further torture was not a repetition, but merely a continuation of the inquiry, designed to make the confessed witch reveal the names of accomplices. For example, in 1597 Clara Geissler, a 69-year-old widow of Gelnhausen in Germany, withstood torture by the thumbscrews, but:

… when her feet were crushed and her body stretched out to greater length, she screamed piteously and said all was true that they demanded of her: she drank the blood of children whom she stole on her night flights, and she had murdered about 60 infants. She named 20 other

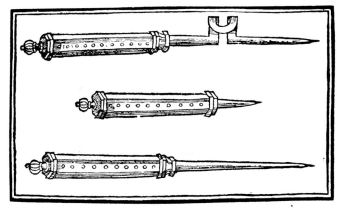

This woodcut from Reginald Scot's The Discoverie of Witchcraft *(1584) shows a genuine bodkin (top), and two false bodkins. These had a spring-loaded blade running into a hollow handle, and when pressed against the victim's flesh, the blade apparently penetrated, but in fact retracted into the handle. The 'witch', therefore, did not cry out in pain, and there was no bleeding.*

women who had been with her at the sabbats, and said the wife of a late burgomaster presided over the flights and banquets.

When she was freed from the rack, Clara retracted her confession saying that she had reported rumours spread by other people. Nevertheless, the judges arrested those she had named, and duly tortured them. One woman confessed even worse crimes than Clara had accused her of, so the widow was submitted to torture once more, to force her to admit the truth. But on her release she again denied her confessions, and was put on the rack again. She was tortured 'with the utmost severity', and died from the agony: the inquiry concluded 'the Devil would not let her reveal anything more, and so wrung her neck'.

The 'preparatory question' was followed by the 'definitive question' and the 'extraordinary question'. The *Malleus Maleficarum* recommended that during the torture, a notary should write down:

Witches were accused of attending a regular 'sabbat', which was said to be presided over by the Devil himself. They were believed to fly through the air to the ceremony, at which all sorts of perverted practices took place.

… everything in his record of the trial, how the prisoner is tortured, on what points he is questioned, and how he answers … If the prisoner will

not confess the truth satisfactorily, other sorts of tortures must be placed before him, with the statement that, unless he will confess the truth, he must endure these also.

Refusing to answer in a judicial inquiry – whether for witchcraft or on any other charge – was in itself a crime that was punishable by death. In witchcraft trials, maintaining silence was regarded not as obstinacy or a sign of strength of character, but as the result of the Devil's charms. In his *Compendium Maleficarum* (1608), Francesco-Maria Guazzo reported that:

> It is a common matter for witches to escape the torture of the rack; for they overcome all the pain by laughter or sleep or silence … A woman of 50 endured boiling fat poured over her whole body, and severe racking of all her limbs, without feeling anything. For she was taken from the rack free from any sense of pain, whole and uninjured, except that her great toe, which had been torn off during her questioning, was not restored, but this did not hinder or hurt her at all. After she had undergone every torture and had obstinately denied all her crimes, she cut her throat in prison. So the Devil, having accused her of witchcraft through the mouth of a possessed woman, killed her.

'A woman of 50 endured boiling fat poured over her whole body, and severe racking of all her limbs'

Associated with this concept was the idea of the 'Devil's mark'. When Isabella Pardea, of Epinal in France, was hauled before the magistrate in 1588, she showed him a mark on her body that she said had been branded by the Devil. 'It occurred to the magistrate to test the truth of this alleged insensitiveness to pain. So he ordered a pin to be thrust and pressed deeply into her, and this was done in the presence of sufficient witnesses, and no blood flowed from the wound, and the witch gave not the least sign of pain.'

The *Malleus Maleficarum* also discusses the question of whether a judge should promise favours or even immunity to a prisoner in order to secure a confession, and whether he should keep his promise. It suggests three courses of conduct. A promise to spare the prisoner's life can be made, without mentioning that the alternative is a sentence of life imprisonment. Or 'for a period the promise made to the sentenced witch is to be kept, but after that time she should be burned'. The third course is for the judge in question to excuse himself from the trial, and for another to sentence the witch to burning.

Should a sick person be tortured? The answer was first to restore the prisoner to health. The quickest way was to throw boiling water under the armpits. Alternatively, the feet could be placed on a fire, so that the prisoner broke out in floods of sweat; this sweat, pouring from every pore in the body, would carry away the disease, and the prisoner would be induced to speak the truth. Pregnant women were spared torture and execution, but only until a month after the birth of the child.

The *Malleus Maleficarum* also warned against the possible suicide of a prisoner. Since suicide itself was a crime, it was obviously due to the persuasions – or even the personal intervention – of the Devil, who had promised that the witch would not die at the stake and was anxious that his promise should be kept.

As the introduction to the bull of Innocent VIII makes clear, it was the persistence of witchcraft in northern Germany that had provoked the original publication of the *Malleus Maleficarum*. Here, and in Switzerland, there had been numerous trials for witchcraft during the fifteenth century, but what provoked the subsequent epidemic of witch-hunts was the spreading belief in the sabbat – the banquet where witches were supposed to gather and worship the Devil. Hence the insistence of the inquisitors upon the use of torture, not only to secure a confession, but to induce the victims to reveal the names of other witches.

Germany, within the Holy Roman Empire, comprised at that time as many as 300 autonomous or semi-autonomous states. In theory, they all subscribed to the Carolina Code of law introduced in 1532 by the emperor, Charles V, under which most of the German witchcraft trials were conducted, and which derived from an earlier edict published in Bamberg in 1502. The code distinguished 'those who tell fortunes by sorcery' from witches: it expressly stated that they were not to be imprisoned or put to torture on mere indictment. On the other hand:

> If anyone teaches others witchcraft; or if he misleads persons into bewitching and in addition brings those he has deceived to effect bewitchment; also if he has associated with witches, either male or female; or with such suspected things, actions, words, and ways as imply witchcraft; and moreover if he is defamed by these same witches: these indications give just proof of witchcraft, and sufficient grounds for torture ...
>
> If someone has done injury or damage to persons through witchcraft, she must be punished from life to death, and this punishment must be by burning.

The publication of the Carolina Code was contemporary with the emergence of Protestantism in the German states, and the spread of

In the course of two centuries, at least 100,000 people were burned in Germany as witches.

witch persecution can be attributed, at least in part, to the fears of the Roman Catholic Church that it was being attacked from within. However, it is remarkable that, even as Protestantism was officially adopted by various states, the hysteria continued, and many states were even more vicious in their attempts to root out witchcraft than those that remained Catholic.

In the course of two centuries, at least 100,000 people were burned in Germany as witches. At Quedlinburg, in Saxony, 133 witches were burned in a single day in 1589. In 1590 a contemporary chronicler wrote of Wolfenbüttel in Brunswick: 'the place of execution looked like a small wood, from the number of stakes'. Forty years later, Cardinal Albizzi paid a visit to Cologne and reported: 'A horrible spectacle met our eyes. Outside the walls of many towns and villages, we saw numerous stakes to which poor wretched women were bound and burned as witches.' At Neisse in Silesia in the 1650s, the executioner built an oven in which, over nine years, he roasted to death more than a thousand people, including children as young as two years of age.

A broadside newsletter describing the burning of three women for witchcraft, at Derneburg in the Harz Mountains, Germany, in October 1555.

Between the Counter Reformation of 1570 and the end of the Thirty Years' War in 1648, many regions changed their official religion more than once. In 1573, the judges at Hagenau in Alsace were Protestant, and a woman charged with witchcraft was spared torture, and freed. Four years later, she was charged again, and this time her judges were Catholic. The trial lasted a year, and she was tortured seven times before she at last confessed, and was burned. On the other hand, the Lutheran Benedict Carpzov is said to have signed the death warrants of 20,000 witches in the first half of the seventeenth century.

The witch-hunt epidemic soon spread to other European countries. In France, isolated cases had occurred as early as 1245, and the burning of Angèle de la Barthe by the inquisitor at Toulouse in 1275 has been claimed as the first execution specifically for witchcraft. France could also claim the first secular trial, when Jehenne de Brigue was arraigned in Paris in October 1390.

Her trial dragged on for nearly a year, having been adjourned when it was thought that she was pregnant, and it was not until August 1391 that she was put to torture by being stripped naked and bound to a ladder. She immediately confessed that she had attempted to poison Jehan de Ruilly, her accuser, in collaboration with his wife Macette. After being racked, Macette agreed that the charge was true. Two weeks of legal argument followed before the Paris *parlement* decided that this was a civil matter, and that the two women could be burned alive as sorcerers. The sentence was carried out on 19 August 1391.

Nicholas Remy, the attorney-general of Lorraine, personally condemned 900 witches

However, most of the purging of witches in fifteenth- and sixteenth-century France was performed by the Inquisition, and it was not until the 1580s that civil judges began to engage in mass persecution. Between 1581 and 1591, Nicholas Rémy, the attorney-general of Lorraine, personally condemned 900 witches; many were burned at Rouen in Normandy between 1589 and 1645; and in Burgundy some 600 were executed on the orders of Henri Boguet, the chief judge of St-Claude. In the Basque country of Labourde, the judge Pierre de Lancre, on the orders of the king, is said to have burned a similar number of witches in four months during 1609.

De Lancre claimed that all 30,000 inhabitants of the region had been infected by devils driven out of Japan and the East Indies by Christian missionaries. He tortured many to confess, and relied heavily upon the testimony of young children. According to his account, when the last witch was burned at the stake, a swarm of toads was seen escaping from her head.

A virtual end to trials for witchcraft in France came with the edict of Louis XIV in 1682, which represented his response to two very different court cases. In 1670, 525 persons had been charged with witchcraft in Rouen, and 12 had already been sentenced to the stake – with another 34 awaiting confirmation of sentence – when their families appealed to the king. He rescinded the sentences, despite vehement protests on the part of the Normandy *parlement*.

Then, in 1678, a fortune-teller, Catherine Deshayes – known as La Voisin – was accused of poisoning before the *Chambre ardente* in Paris. The police Commissioner Reynie submitted her to torture, using first

Burning a woman found guilty of practising witchcraft, in Amsterdam. She is not tied to an upright stake, which was the usual method. Instead, strapped to a ladder, she is flung forward into a pyre that has already been lit.

the *sellette* (the torture chair), and then the *brodequins* – iron boots into which wedges were hammered to crush her legs. Despite excruciating pain, La Voisin denied all charges of poisoning. The attorney-general requested that her tongue should be cut out, and her hands chopped from her wrists, but the court committed her to the stake. On 22 February 1680 she was 'tied and bound with iron. Cursing all the time, she was covered with straw, which five or six times she threw off her, but at last the flames grew fiercer, and she was lost to sight.'

Judicial inquiries revealed that, in fact, La Voisin's house had been used for the celebration of Black Masses, and that a considerable number of the most distinguished members of the royal circle, including the king's mistress, Madame de Montespan, had been involved. Reynie continued his inquiries for two more years, torturing and burning many of the lower classes, but not the noble principals. Some years later Louis ordered the records to be destroyed.

It was because of this embarrassing event, and to put an end to trials for witchcraft, that the king issued his historic edict. Aimed principally at the suppression of fortune-telling, it defined witchcraft as no more than 'superstition, supposed magic, pretence' – still a crime, but no longer warranting torture and the stake. Most of the provincial *parlements* submitted to the royal will, although it was 1718 before the last witch was burned in Bordeaux.

In England, the persecution of witches started later than in Europe, and did not last nearly as long. Until well into the sixteenth century, the punishments for witchcraft were relatively light – sometimes no more than an hour or two in the pillory, and the promise not to sin again. In 1542, toward the end of the reign of Henry VIII, the first law specifically against witchcraft was passed; but five years later, under Edward VI, this statute was repealed. After Elizabeth came to the throne in 1558 concern grew about the dangers of witchcraft: the queen felt vulnerable to all sorts of plots, particularly those of Catholic Spain, and any kind of sorcery was regarded as a threat to her existence.

The obsession with witch-hunts may well have been due to the return to England of 472 leading Protestant exiles who had personally seen the burning of witches in Strasbourg, Frankfurt, Zurich, Geneva, or Berne. In 1560, Bishop John Jewel delivered a sermon before Elizabeth:

The Hexenhaus *(witch-house) of Bamberg, Germany, was a notorious prison during the persecution of witches. Here an elderly woman, due for interrogation, is strapped in iron fetters, and chained to the wall.*

… that kind of people (I mean witches and sorcerers) within these last few years are marvellously increased within your Grace's realm. These eyes have seen most evident and manifest marks of their wickedness. Your Grace's subjects pine away even unto death, their colour fadeth, their flesh rotteth, their speech is benumbed, their senses are bereft. Wherefore, your poor subjects' most humble petition unto your Highness is that the laws touching such malefactors may be put in due execution.

The result was the Act of 1563, 'against conjurations, enchantments and witchcrafts'. The penalties defined by this Act were relatively mild – murder by sorcery was naturally punishable by death, but practising witches were subject only to the pillory and a year's imprisonment, and property was only forfeit on a second offence – and there was no legalization of torture. Nevertheless, this statute inaugurated a century of witch-hunts in England.

In principle, torture remained forbidden under English law, although in cases of treason a licence could be obtained from the monarch, the Privy Council, or the Star Chamber. However, there were no regulations concerning the conditions under which prisoners could be confined. They could be shut up in a stinking hole infested with rats; they could be refused food and water and prevented from sleeping. And, since the instruments of torture existed, they could be shown them and threatened with their use. These methods were usually sufficient to obtain an acceptable form of confession. Nevertheless, in the midst of this brutality, there was a kind of charity: witches were not burned alive at the stake in England, but hanged.

The nearest approach to the torture of witches in England came in the years 1645 to 1646, when Matthew Hopkins, the self-proclaimed 'Witch Finder General', carried out his inquiries in East Anglia. Hopkins's favourite method of extorting confessions was the 'swimming' of witches. He took his justification from the *Demonology* (1597) of James VI of Scotland (subsequently James I of England):

> So it appears that God hath appointed, for a supernatural sign of the monstrous impiety of the witches, that the water shall refuse to receive them in her bosom, that have shaken off them the sacred water of baptism and willfully refused benefit thereof.

The procedure involved tying the right thumb to the left big toe, and immersing the witches in water. If they floated, they were guilty. If they sank, they were innocent – but they very likely drowned. In the summer of 1645, an English parliamentary commission condemned the practice, and Hopkins was forced to find other methods. He resorted to forcing his prisoners to sit cross-legged on a stool for many hours, or making them continue to walk about their cell for four or five days without sleep. One of his victims was a 70-year-old parson, Rev John Lowes. A succession of Hopkins's assistants:

> ... kept him awake several nights together, and ran him backwards and forwards about the room until he was out of breath. Then they rested him a little and then ran him again. And thus they did for several days

there was a kind of charity: witches were not burned alive at the stake in England, but hanged

and nights together, till he was weary of his life and was scarce sensible of what he said or did.

In this state, it is not surprising that Lowes confessed to making a covenant with the Devil, bewitching cattle, and sinking a ship off Harwich.

Hopkins was particularly taken with the idea of the Devil's mark, and 'discovered' many witches by pricking them with a bodkin on a mole, birthmark, or scar to see whether they bled or cried out in pain. During Hopkins's 18 months as a professional witch-finder, demand for his pricking services was so great that he and his partner, John Stearns, hired four assistants to go from village to village and seek out likely victims. It seems probable that they made use of a fake bodkin with a spring-loaded handle, into which the blade slid as it was apparently forced into the alleged witch's flesh. Hopkins was compelled to retire in the summer of 1646, and died of tuberculosis within the year.

The crime of witchcraft was brought into Scottish law in 1563, the same year as in England, by Mary Stuart. Following this, there were a number of trials, and witches found guilty were burned, but the persecution of witches did not really take hold until the reign of Mary's son James (VI of Scotland, and subsequently also I of England). It began with the case of the witches of North Berwick.

In 1590 David Seaton, deputy bailiff of Tranent, a small town 16km (10 miles) from Edinburgh, became suspicious of the activities of his young servant Gilly Duncan. He tortured her, using 'the pilliwinks [a sort of thumbscrew] upon her fingers, which is a grievous torture; and binding and wrenching her head with a cord, or rope, which is a most cruel torment also'. But Gilly would not confess anything, until Seaton searched her for the Devil's mark, which he claimed to have found on her throat; she then confessed to 'the wicked allurements and enticements of the Devil'.

Confined to prison, she soon named a number of accomplices involved, she said, not only in witchcraft but in a diabolical plot against King James. Among those

'Swimming' an old woman to determine whether she is a witch. Victims of this treatment seldom survived. If they floated, they were deemed guilty, and hanged. And if they sank, indicating that they were innocent – they usually drowned.

she implicated were a respectable midwife, Agnes Sampson; John Fian, a schoolmaster; and two 'reputed for as civil honest women as any that dwelled within the city of Edinburgh' – Euphemia Maclean, the daughter of Lord Cliftonhall, and Barbara Napier. And the instigator of the plot, she said, was Francis Hepburn, Earl of Bothwell and the king's cousin, who had some claim to the throne if James died without an heir.

The hanging of four women found guilty of witchcraft, at Chelmsford, Essex, in 1645. The figure at the right, labelled 'D', is Matthew Hopkins, receiving payment for his activities.

Agnes Sampson was examined at Holyrood by James himself. Having denied all 53 charges against her, she was shaved, and every part of her body searched until the Devil's mark was found. Then she was chained to the wall of her cell with a 'witch's bridle', an iron frame with four prongs that were forced inside the mouth, two against the tongue and two against the cheeks. Denied sleep, she too was tortured with a rope about her head, until she confessed.

Most of the charges related to simple folk magic, such as curing disease by charms, but finally Agnes broke down and told how on Allhallows Eve 1589 she and a crowd of women, and six men, had sailed in sieves from Leith to North Berwick for a great merrymaking. There they had cast a spell to raise a great storm that would sink the king's ship as he returned to Scotland after his marriage to Anne of Denmark.

Barbara Napier and Euphemia Maclean subsequently told a similar tale, and named John Fian as the recorder of the Devil's instructions. He in turn implicated Bothwell in his confession, but then retracted (after he had been visited in his cell by – it has been suggested – Bothwell himself), and despite further torture refused to say another word.

Fian and Agnes Sampson were strangled, and then burnt. Euphemia Maclean was denied this mercy and 'burned in ashes alive to the death'. Barbara Napier pleaded pregnancy, and, after some time, 'she was set at liberty'. After several attempts to kidnap James, Bothwell eventually fled from Scotland and took refuge in Italy.

With the discovery of this plot, James became convinced of the existence of witchcraft, and in 1597 he published his book *Demonology*. When he became King of England in 1603, on the death of Elizabeth, he brought out a new edition of the book in London. And in 1604 he ordered the passing of a new English statute on witchcraft that equated it with a pact with the Devil, as in other European countries. However, the personal interest that he took in a number of cases that followed soon after the passing of this law gradually changed his opinion, and by the end of his reign he was a convinced sceptic.

Nevertheless, in Scotland the persecution of witches continued, so much so that the country soon rivalled Germany in the number of executions and the horrors of the torture chamber. In June 1596, Alison Balfour of Orkney, 'a known notorious witch', was bound for two days in the 'cashielaws' (a kind of iron vice). While she endured this, she had to watch her 81-year-old husband pressed under 318kg (700lb) of iron, her son placed in the 'Spanish boots', where nearly 60 blows were given to wedges to reduce his legs to pulp, and her young daughter subjected to the pilliwinks. Her servant, Thomas Palpa, was 'kept in the cashielaws 11 days and 11 nights; twice in the day, for the space of 14 days, placed in the boots, he being naked in the mean time; and scourged with the tawse in court, that they left neither flesh nor hide on him'.

In 1618, at Irvine in Ayrshire, Margaret Barclay, the wife of a burgess of the town, was charged with the sinking of a ship by witchcraft; and a

A print from a contemporary pamphlet describing the trial of the North Berwick witches for conspiring the sinking of the ship carrying King James VI of Scotland (later James I of England). At the left, John Fian sits at a desk, taking down the Devil's instructions.

vagrant, John Stewart, was charged with precognition of the event. He implicated an accomplice, Isobel Insh, and her eight-year-old daughter. Isobel was tortured until she confessed, but managed to escape from the belfry of the church where she was confined and fell from the roof to her death. John Stewart contrived to strangle himself with the strings of his bonnet, but Margaret was then put to what the Earl of Eglinton called 'a most safe and gentle torture' – by setting 'her two bare legs in a pair of stocks, and thereafter by on-laying of certain iron bars'. When she could stand no more, she cried: 'Take off! take off! and before God I shall show you the whole form.' At her trial, however, she recanted: 'All I have confessed was in agony of torture, and before God all I have spoken is false and untrue' – but she was, nevertheless, convicted, strangled, and burned.

During the torture, Margaret had implicated a fourth person, Isobel Crawford. She too did 'admirably, without any kind of din or exclamation, suffer above 30 stone [190kg] of iron to be laid on her legs, never shrinking thereat in any sort, but remaining, as it were, steady'. She at last confessed what was asked of her, but also denied everything when released, and died maintaining that she was innocent.

In 1652, two fugitives from Scotland told an English commission how, with four other accused – who had died under the torture – they had been hung by their thumbs, whipped, and burned between the toes, in the mouth, and on the head.

Belief in witchcraft persisted in Scotland into the eighteenth century. At Pittenweem in Fifeshire, in 1705, one 16-year-old Patrick Morton accused Beatrix Laing, Isobel Adam, Janet Cornfoot, and others, of bewitching him. Beatrix Laing was tortured, and then confined alone in a dark dungeon for five months. She was finally released on payment of a fine, but was driven from the town, and died of her injuries. Isobel Adam also escaped with a fine, but Janet Cornfoot was seized by a mob and dragged on a rope to the harbour. There she was strung between the shore and a boat, swung back and forth, and pelted with stones. Finally she was crushed to death beneath a door piled with rocks – 'and to be sure it was so, they called a man with a horse and a sledge, and made him drive over her corpse backward and forward several times'.

The last known execution for witchcraft in Scotland occurred in 1727. The total number of witches executed has been discussed by several writers. One reported that the Scottish presbytery had admitted the burning of some 4000, and an article in the *Scottish Review* of 1891 gave details of 3400 between 1590 and 1680. In 1938, George Black named 1800 witches, and he estimated a total of 4400.

'they called a man with a horse and a sledge, and made him drive over her corpse'

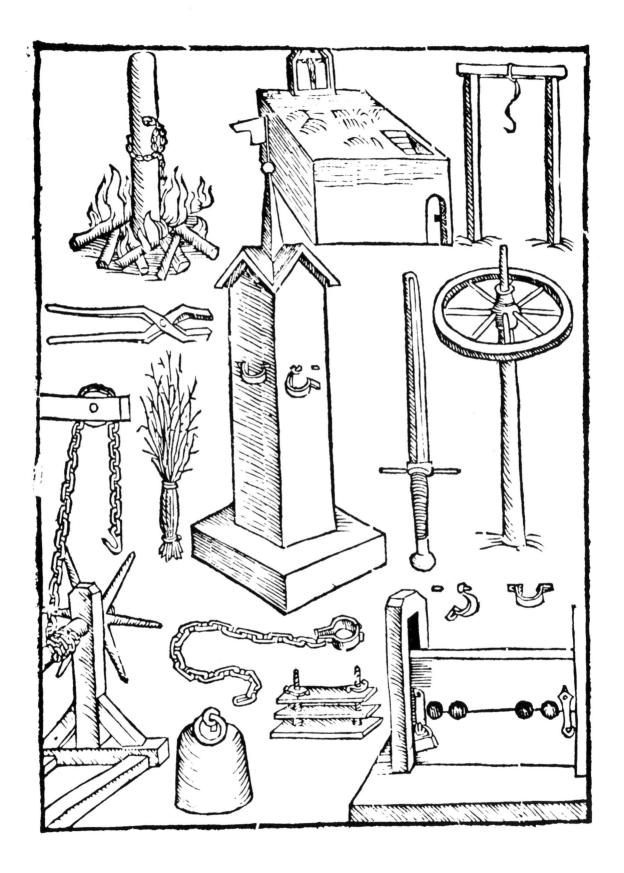

Chapter Eight

Instruments of Torture

Purely physical torture, by beating and flogging, by fire or by water, was not enough for the more sadistic interrogators, who demanded ingenious instruments specifically designed to inflict exquisite pain – pain that could, at the same time, be gradually increased to extract further confessions.

The rack

Probably the most infamous, and the most widely employed, instrument of torture was the rack. Its use goes back to antiquity. There is an ancient Greek legend of the bandit Procrustes, who haunted one of the roads leading to Athens. He had a bed made of iron, and all those who were unfortunate enough to fall into his hands were placed on it. If they were longer than the bed, Procrustes cut off the overhanging parts – head or feet, he was indifferent – and threw the pieces over the cliff to a giant tortoise that lived below. If, however, they were too short, he stretched them until they fitted. He was eventually killed by the legendary hero Theseus.

We know from a passage in Aristophanes's *The Frogs* (c. 406 BC) (see Chapter 1, page 15), that the rack was used as a means of civil torture in Greek legal inquiries. It was also used by the Roman emperors, notably Tiberius (see Chapter 1, page 18), but the details of its construction at that time are unknown.

However, although many variations of the rack have been used throughout the centuries, the basic principle has always been the same. Victims' hands are secured by ropes to a beam at one end, and their bodies gradually stretched by ropes attached to their feet. At first, they resist the stretching, not only with the muscles of their arms and legs, but also with their abdominal muscles. Then, suddenly, the muscles of their limbs give way, first in the arms and subsequently in the legs: the ligaments, and then the fibres of the muscles themselves, are torn. Further stretching ruptures the muscles of the abdomen, and, if the torture is continued, the limbs will be dislocated, and finally torn from their sockets.

(Opposite) An early woodcut of many of the instruments of torture employed in interrogations in Germany during the 15th century. A primitive form of the thumbscrews appears to be illustrated at bottom centre.

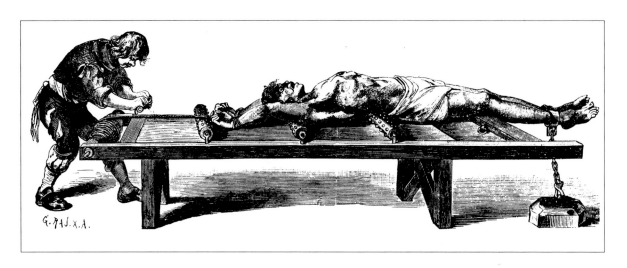

A form of the rack – one that was particularly popular in Germany – caused the victim to be not only stretched, but drawn at the same time over a succession of studded rollers.

The torture of the Christian martyr Quintinus is described in John Foxe's *Book of Martyrs*:

Then the Prefect, raging with despotic fury, ordered the holy Quintinus to be so cruelly racked at the pulleys that his limbs were forced apart at the joints from sheer violence. Moreover, he commanded him to be beaten with small cords, and boiling oil and pitch and melted fat to be poured over him, that no kind of punishment or torment might fail to add to his bodily anguish.

From Roman times until the early Middle Ages, there are few records of the use of the rack, but it was increasingly employed – principally by the civil authorities – from the time of the institution of the Inquisition (see Chapter 3, page 49). It was known as the *chevalet* (little horse) in France, the *escalera* (ladder) in Spain, and the *Folter* (frame) in Germany. It was said to have been introduced to England about 1420 by John Holland, Duke of Exeter, when he was Constable of the Tower.

At that time, the rack could be either vertical or horizontal. It consisted of an open, rectangular, wooden or iron frame, something over 2m (6ft) in length. In the vertical position, the victims' wrists were fastened to the upper beam. The ropes attached to their feet were then gradually loaded with weights, or alternatively led over a windlass at the other end of the frame, which was turned by two torturers.

In the horizontal position, the frame was raised about a metre (three feet) from the floor. Victims were laid on the floor within it, and ropes led from their wrists and ankles over a beam or windlass at either end.

(Other forms of the rack had battens across the frame, on which the victims lay: this accounts for it often being known as the 'ladder'.) Weights could be attached to all four ropes, but the preferred method was to wind the ropes on the two windlasses. This required the efforts of four men. They were provided with poles, which they inserted into holes in the ends of the windlasses. One man at each end would keep the rope taut, while his fellow torturer inserted his pole into the next hole in the windlass, and wound on. At first, victims would be raised from the ground until, with every muscle straining, they lay horizontal between the windlasses; then the torture continued.

The next development was to provide the windlass at each end of the rack with a ratchet mechanism. In this way, the tension of the ropes was maintained after each turn of the windlass, and only two men were needed to operate the rack. Later, the ropes were led around a single, central wooden roller with a ratchet at each end, so that the torture could be carried out by just one man. Although it was stipulated that there should always be independent witnesses present to hear the confessions wrung from the victims, there are implications that, frequently, only the torturer was present – and what he alone reported of a confession was deemed to be sufficient to secure a conviction.

Sometimes, victims were attached to the rack by their thumbs and big toes. A French account describes the interrogation of a certain Pierre Delluque, accused of stealing a mare. Even after the rack had been turned through 12 cogs, he insisted that he was innocent:

Sometimes victims were attached to the rack by their thumbs and big toes.

> Thereupon ordered ... three more cogs to be turned, and the accused, interrogated, answered that the Devil might take him, body and soul, if he had been a party to any robbery. And, having ordered three more cogs to be turned, again interrogated the accused as to the above facts, but he made no reply.
>
> Thereupon called upon the surgeons who ... reported that breathing was suspended, and he was in danger of suffocation unless released within a few moments.
>
> On this report, ordered the accused to be released, he having regained consciousness by the aid of cordials administered by the surgeons. Interrogated again, but still denied being a party to any robbery. Thereupon, having ordered the cords to be stretched again to the same point as before, the accused, interrogated again, replied only with loud screams; and having ordered the executioner to turn two more cogs, the accused still gave no reply, and the surgeons, having again examined the state of the accused, reported that the movement of the diaphragm was

stopped by the twisting of the nerves, and the thumb of his right hand was torn off, and that he was in danger of losing his life …

Thereupon ordered the executioner to entirely loosen the accused; had him carried on a mattress before a fire, where he regained consciousness with the help of the surgeons, and the cordials they administered him. Read over to him the present report, and after interrogating him generally as to all the facts, he again answered that he had not committed any robbery either alone or with accomplices.

A French variant of the horizontal rack was the wheel. Victims were strapped to its circumference with their hands tied in advance of their heads, and their feet fettered to the floor. As the wheel was turned, they were stretched, just as on the rack.

A rather different form of rack was used by some German authorities. Victims were subjected to stretching, while their arms and legs were bound to the sides of the framework with thin cords. These were wound three times round their limbs, and a stick was inserted between each cord and the frame. As the sticks were turned, the cords gradually

A different type of rack, similar to that on which John Coustos suffered at the hands of the Inquisition in Lisbon in 1743. As the ropes and chains are tightened across his chest and round his wrists, the victim suffers excruciating agony.

tightened, until they bit through the unfortunate victim's flesh.

The Englishman John Coustos, who fell into the hands of the Inquisition in Lisbon in 1743, suffered the same fate. He was accused of being a Freemason, and ordered to reveal the secrets of freemasonry. He was laid on the rack on his back with his neck in an iron collar, and his feet were fastened with ropes drawn tightly through two iron rings. Two ropes the thickness of a little finger were wound around each arm and leg, and passed through holes in each side of the rack framework. Four times the executioners tightened the ropes, until Coustos fainted from pain and loss of blood. He was then taken back to his dungeon.

Six weeks later, when his wounds were partly healed, Coustos was brought back to the torture chamber. This time he was bound to a different type of rack. He was made to stretch his arms horizontally behind him, fastened so that the palms of his hands were turned outward. The rack gradually drew his arms together until the backs of his hands touched. Both shoulders were dislocated, and blood gushed from his mouth. He still kept silent, and was carried to the dungeon, where surgeons reset his bones.

Two months later he was tortured again. He was made to stand against a strong wooden wall, at each end of which was a pulley. A chain was wound twice round his stomach, and ended in rings fastened to his wrists. Ropes were attached to these rings, and led through pulleys to a roller. As the roller was turned his arms were gradually dragged once more from their sockets, and at the same time the chain bit deeply into his naked flesh. Despite this fearful torture, Coustos still refused to divulge the secrets of freemasonry. The incident caused an outcry in England, and led to diplomatic intervention.

One of many women who were also tortured by the Portuguese Inquisition was Jane Bohorquia:

> This young creature was carried out to torture and, on being returned to it from jail, she was so shaken, and had all her limbs so miserably disjointed on the rack, that when she lay on her bed of rushes it rather increased her misery than gave her rest, so that she could not turn without pain.
>
> She had scarcely begun to recover from her torture, when she was carried back to the same exercise, and was tortured with such diabolic cruelty on the rack, that the ropes pierced and cut into the very bones of her arms, thighs, and legs, and in this manner she was brought back into prison, just ready to expire, the blood immediately running out of her mouth in great plenty. Undoubtedly they had burst her bowels, insomuch that the eighth day after her torture, she died.

As the roller was turned his arms were gradually dragged once more from their sockets.

One version of the rack used in Germany was known as the 'Austrian ladder'. This was a wide, ladder-like frame that was leant at an angle against the wall of the torture chamber. Victims were placed halfway up, their backs to the ladder, with their wrists secured to a rung behind them. Ropes attached to their ankles led to a windlass at the foot of the ladder. As this was turned, the arms were drawn up behind them, until both shoulders were dislocated.

Another German variant was a conventional horizontal rack, but with a central spiked roller beneath the back, which turned as the victim was stretched. A similar method was used in Italy: the victim was stretched horizontally, unsupported, and a spike was positioned immediately under the back. This was known as *la veglia* (wakefulness), which is a very appropriate name, as it was necessary constantly to tense the muscles to avoid relaxing on to the spike.

Skeffington's gyves

A device that appears to have been developed and used only in England – although it was effectively a fiendishly ingenious development of the Indian torture of *anundal* (see Chapter 9, page 154) – was known as 'Skeffington's gyves', or sometimes as the 'scavenger's daughter'. Its invention has been attributed to Sir Leonard Skeffington, who was Lieutenant of the Tower during the reign of Henry VIII.

It was a large iron hoop, hinged in two halves. With their hands bound behind them, victims were made to kneel on the lower half. Then the executioner, straddling his back, forced them down and closed the other half with a screw. As the screw was tightened, the body was pressed ever closer together – the chest against the knees, belly against the thighs, thighs against the legs. Gradually, the spine was dislocated, the breastbone and ribs fractured.

Gradually, the spine was dislocated, the breastbone and ribs fractured.

Among those who suffered this dreadful torture during the reign of Elizabeth I were two Jesuits, Thomas Coteham and Lucas Kerbie. John Stowe, a contemporary chronicler, described how they were charged with high treason:

... for that, contrary both to love and dutie, they forsooke their native countrey, to live beyond the seas under the Pope's obedience ... these menne having vowed their alleagiance to the pope, to obey him in all causes whatsoever ... And for this intent and purpose they were sent over to seduce the harts of her Majestie's loving subjects, and to conspire and practise her Grace's death, as much as in them lay, against a great daie, set and appoynted, when the general havocke should be made ...

Coteham and Kerbie were carried to the Tower on 5 December 1580, and subjected to Skeffington's gyves: Coteham, it was reported, 'bled profusely from the nose'. After this they lay in prison for nearly a year until, on 20 November 1581, they were brought to the bar in Westminster, and 'by a jurie they were approved guiltie, and had judgement to bee hanged, bowelled and quartered'.

Another victim was Thomas Miagh, accused of treasonable correspondence with the Irish rebels. He was brought to the Tower on 10 March 1581; one of the Tower's walls still bears his inscription: 'Thomas Miagh which lieth here alone, that Fayne wold from hens be gone, by tortyre straynge mi troyth was tryed, yet of mi Libertie denied'.

This 'tortyre straynge' was the gyves, and it was reported that 'we subjected hym to the tortyr of Skevington's Iron and with so mutche sharpeness as was in our judgement conveniente, yett can we get from hym no farther matter'. Miagh was then handed over to the rackmaster, Thomas Norton, 'to deal with him with the rack in such sort as they should see fit'. But it seems that Miagh could provide no important information, for he was released at the end of the year and returned to Ireland a broken man.

A somewhat similar treatment was employed as a punishment in the Royal Navy during the eighteenth century. It was known as 'tying neck and heels'. Culprits were made to sit on the deck, with a musket under the knees, and another over the neck. The two muskets were then strapped together, so tightly that blood flowed from the nose, mouth, and ears.

A variation of the instrument known as 'Skeffington's gyves', or 'the scavenger's daughter'. Its invention has been attributed to Sir Leonard Skeffington, who was Lieutenant of the Tower during the reign of Henry VIII.

The thumbscrews

A Scottish document of 1684 refers to 'a new inventione and Ingyne called thumbekins', but there are references to the device, under the name of 'pyrowykes', as early as 1397. Its introduction to Scotland is attributed to Thomas Dalyell, who had been imprisoned in the Tower in 1652, but escaped and became a general in the Russian army. When Charles II was restored to the monarchy in 1660, Dalyell returned to Scotland and, it is claimed, brought some Russian thumbscrews back with him.

In its original form as 'pyrowykes' the instrument was no more than a squeezing device like a pair of nutcrackers. In its more sophisticated form it consisted of two short iron bars, one of which had three rods that fitted into three matching holes in the other. The tips of the victim's thumbs or fingers were placed between the bars, each side of the central rod, which could then be screwed tighter and tighter.

Dalyell employed the instrument in his examination of one William Spence: 'Little screws of steel were made use of, that screwed the thumbs with that exquisite torture, that he sunk under this, for he was told that they would screw every joint of his whole body, one after another, till he confessed.'

Under Charles II, the thumbscrews were used in the interrogation of several men accused of conspiracy against the king's life. One of these was William Carstares, a prominent Scottish minister, who was tortured in 1683 in connection with what is known as the Rye House Plot. Bishop Burnet's *History of His Own Time* (1724–34) describes how:

... the executioner with the engines of torture being present, the lord chancellor commanded the bailie to cause the executioner to put him in the torture by applying the thumbscrews on him, which being done, and he having for the space of an hour continued in the agony of torture, the screw being space and space stretched until he appeared near to faint; and they drew him so hard that as they put him to extreme torture, so that they could not unscrew them, till the smith that had made them was brought with his tools to take them off.

Carstares was released after 18 months in prison due to lack of evidence, and later demonstrated the thumbscrews to William III, who became king in 1689. William insisted on trying them, and admitted that they would have made him confess to anything. No doubt with this in mind, he had no hesitation in ordering their use on Henry Neville Payne in a letter to the Privy Council:

Whereas we have full assurance upon undeniable evidence of a horrid plott and conspiracy against our government, and the whole settlement of that our ancient kingdom, for introducing the authoritie of the late King James and Popery in these kingdoms, and setting up an intire new form of government, whereof there has been several contrivers and

A thumbscrew. Thomas Dalyell is said to have introduced this instrument into Scotland, having learnt about its use while he was a general in the Russian army. The Scottish minister William Carstares, having suffered the torture, later demonstrated the thumbscrews to King William III, who said they would have made him confess to anything.

managers, and Nevil Pain, now prisoner in our Castle of Edinburgh, hath lykewayes been an instrument in that conspiracie, wee doe require you to examine Nevil Pain strictly; and in case he prove obstinate or disengenious do you proceed against him to torture, with all the rigour that the law allows in such cases; and not doubting your ready and vigorous applications for the furder discovery of what so much concerns the public safety, we bid you heartily farewell.

Payne, it is said, suffered two days in the thumbscrews, and endured further torture, but he confessed to little and was subsequently sentenced to 10 years in prison.

Thumbscrews were employed in many other European countries. In Germany, they were made even more horrific by being fitted with spikes, which bored into the quick of the victim's nails.

The boots

The torture of the boot was described by those who witnessed it as 'the most severe and cruel pain in the world'. Indeed, as Bishop Burnet wrote: 'When any are to be stuck in the boots, it is done in the presence of the Council, and upon that happening, almost all offer to run away. The sight is so dreadful that, without an order restraining such a number to stay, the press boards would remain unused.'

Although the torture was known as the 'boot' or 'boots', the term 'press boards' more accurately describes the commonest form of the device. The victim was seated on a bench, and boards were placed on the inside and outside of each leg. These boards – described as 'not unlike the short cases we use to guard young trees from the rabbits' – were bound tightly together. Wedges of wood or metal were then driven between the centre boards with a mallet. For the 'ordinary' torture, four wedges were used; eight were employed in the 'extraordinary' torture. The pain was excruciating, and the bones of the victim's legs were frequently splintered or broken.

In France, a similar device was known as the *brodequin*. The name comes from a calf-length laced boot that was worn by actors; in England, the same type of boots were known as 'buskins'. The *brodequin*, as an instrument of torture, was a boot-shaped wooden box that was large enough to contain both legs. Wedges were driven between the victim's legs or knees. This was the method of torture employed in the interrogation of Francis Ravaillac, who assassinated Henri IV of France in 1589, in an attempt to discover whether there had been any fellow-conspirators:

For the 'ordinary' torture, four wedges were used; eight were employed in the 'extraordinary' torture.

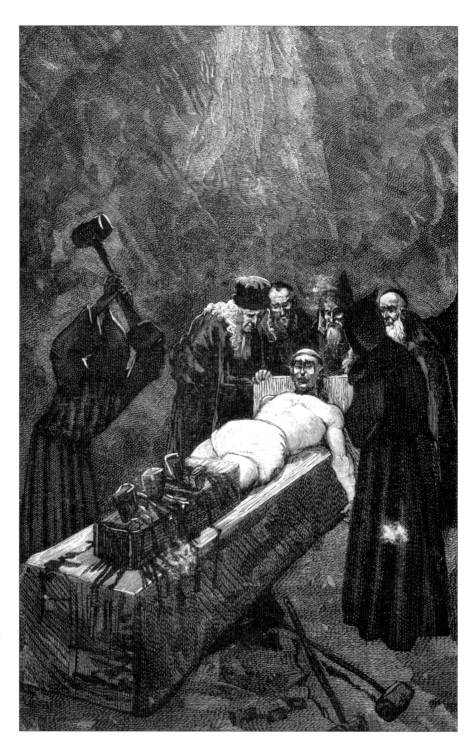

Father Urbain Grandier was accused of making a pact with the Devil, and bewitching a number of nuns, at Loudun, France, in 1633. He suffered the brodequin – *'so severe that the marrow of his bones oozed out of his broken limbs'.*

Ravaillac was then ordered to be put to the torture of the *brodequin* and, the first wedge being driven, he cried out 'God have mercy upon my soul, and pardon the crime I have committed; I never disclosed my intention to anyone' …

When the second wedge was driven, he said with loud cries and shrieks 'I am a sinner, I know no more than I have declared, by the oath I have taken, and by the truth I owe to God and the Court … I beseech the Court not to drive my soul to despair.'.

The executioner continuing to drive the second wedge, he cried out 'My God, receive this penance as an expiation for the greater crimes I have committed in this world; oh God, I accept these torments in satisfaction for my sins …'.

The third wedge was now driven lower, near his feet … and he fainted away. The executioner forced some wine into his mouth, but he could not swallow it and, being quite speechless, he was released from the torture, and water thrown on his face and hands. Some wine being forced down his throat, his speech returned, and he was laid on a mattress in the same place, where he continued till noon.

the first wedge being driven, he cried out 'God have mercy upon my soul, and pardon the crime I have committed'

Finally, after further torment, Ravaillac was then torn to pieces by four horses. In Scotland a similar device was apparently made of iron. It was used in the interrogation of John Spreull, who was accused at Edinburgh in 1681 of a plot to blow up the Duke of York (the future James II of England, VII of Scotland). James himself was present in the torture chamber, along with Thomas Dalyell and other notabilities:

The hangman put [Spreull's] foot in the instrument called the Boot, and, at every query put to him, gave five strokes or thereby upon the wedges … When nothing could be expiscated by this, they ordered the old boot to be brought, alleging this new one used by the hangman was not so good as the old, and accordingly it was brought, and he underwent the torture a second time, and adhered to what he had before said. General Dalyell complained at the second torture, that the hangman did not strike strongly enough upon the wedges; he said, he struck with all his strength, and offered the general the mall to do it himself.
History of the Sufferings of the Church of Scotland,
Robert Wodrow, 1828

Women also suffered this treatment. On 1 February 1631, the Scottish Privy Council ordered: 'Margaret Wod to be putt to the tortour of the bootes, the morne, at ten of the clocke, in the Laich Counsell

Hous of Edinburgh; and that the whole counsell be present when the tortour is given.'

A further sadistic refinement was the notorious 'Spanish boot', which was used in many countries, including Scotland. This, too, was made of iron, but it was fitted with a screw mechanism to compress the calf of the leg. If the victim endured this without breaking down, the boot was gradually heated in a charcoal brazier, until the pain became too agonizing to bear.

Subtle variations of this treatment were practised in France. One method made use of high boots made of a soft, spongy leather. The victim, wearing the boots, was put close to a hot fire, and boiling water was poured into the boots. Another method involved the victim being made to put on wet stockings which were made of parchment. When the unfortunate victim was placed in front of a fire, the parchment consequently dried and shrank, resulting in excruciating pain that spread throughout the whole of both legs.

The victim was put close to a hot fire, and boiling water was poured into the boots.

The Iron Maiden
No more diabolical 'engine of torment' was ever devised than the device known variously as the Iron Maiden, the 'Virgin', or, in German, the *Jungfer*. A certain Colonel Lehmanowsky claimed to have seen it in Madrid, and reported that it 'surpassed all other in fiendish ingenuity'. Its existence was the subject only of rumour, since apparently no specimen of the instrument survived, and during the early nineteenth century it was believed to be a myth. However, in 1832 Dr Mayer, the keeper of the archives at Nuremberg, confirmed that such an apparatus had previously been used in the castle there. Eventually a specimen was unearthed in a collection of antiquities that was owned by Baron Diedrich, and was subsequently described in the English publication *Archaeologia* in 1838.

It had a conical body constructed of sheet iron, topped with a female head wearing a bonnet and ruff, and stood on a wooden base. The front opened with two doors, through which the victim was backed into the Maiden's embrace. Protruding from the inside of one door were 13 square-sectioned spikes, and from the other a further eight. These were positioned so that, as the doors were gradually closed, they pierced the victim's vital organs, and another two were set at face level, in order to pierce the eyes.

A similar instrument, which may well have been the device reported by Colonel Lehmanowsky, was very like that attributed to the Greek tyrant Nabis (see Chapter 1, page 16). It was described in *The Percy*

Anecdotes (1820–23), and subsequently in Frederic Shoberl's *Persecutions of Popery* (1844):

On the entry of the French into Toledo, during the Peninsular War [1808], General Lasalle visited the palace of the Inquisition. The great number of the instruments of torture, especially the instruments to stretch the limbs … excited horror even in the minds of soldiers hardened in the field of battle. One of these instruments, singular in its kind for refined torture, and disgraceful to reason and religion in the choice of its object, deserved a particular description.

In a subterranean vault, adjoining the secret audience chamber, stood … a wooden statue made by the hands of monks, and representing the Virgin Mary. A gilded glory encompassed her head, and in her right hand she held a banner. It struck us all, at first sight, that, notwithstanding the silken robe, descending on each side in ample folds from her shoulders, she should wear a sort of cuirass. On closer scrutiny, it appeared that the forepart of the body was stuck full of extremely sharp nails and narrow knife-blades, with the points of both turned toward the spectator.

The arms and hands were jointed; and machinery behind the partition set the figure in motion. One of the servants of the Inquisition was compelled, by command of the General, to work the machine, as he termed it. When the figure extended her arms, as though to press someone most lovingly to her heart, the well-filled knapsack of a Polish grenadier was made to supply the place of a living victim.

The statue hugged it closer and closer; and, when the attendant, agreeably to orders, made the figure unclasp her arms and return to her former position, the knapsack was perforated to the depth of two or three inches [five to seven centimetres], and remained hanging on

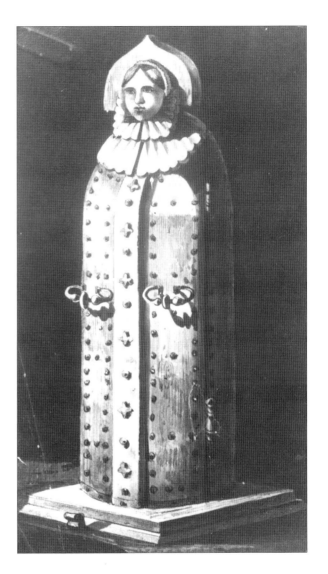

The infamous Iron Maiden, or 'Virgin of Nuremberg'.

the points of the nails and knife-blades. One of the familiars, as they are called, of the Inquisition gave us an account of the customary mode of proceeding on using the machine. The substance of his report was as follows:

'Persons accused of heresy, or of blaspheming God or the Saints, and obstinately refusing to confess their guilt, were conducted into this cellar, at the further end of which numerous lamps, placed round a recess, threw a variegated light on the gilded glory, and on the head of the figure and the flag in her right hand. At a little altar, standing opposite to her, and hung with black, the prisoner received the sacrament; and two ecclesiastics earnestly admonished him, in the presence of the Mother of God, to make a confession. "See," said they, "how lovingly the blessed Virgin opens her arms to thee! on her bosom thy hardened heart will be melted; there wilt thou confess." All at once, the figure began to raise extended arms: the prisoner, overwhelmed with astonishment, was led to her embrace; she drew him nearer and nearer, pressed him almost imperceptibly closer and closer, till the spikes and knives pierced his breast.'

'she drew him nearer and nearer till the spikes and knives pierced his breast'

The iron chair

The use of the gridiron has been described in Chapter 4 (see page 61), and the use of the 'Spanish', or iron, chair in Chapter 5 (see page 72). The latter had earlier been employed by the Romans in the torture of Christians:

It was commanded that seven seats of brass be brought in, and the women, seven in number, who, during the torment of Saint Blase, had collected the holy drops of blood which fell from him, to sit thereon, one in each. Then were the said seats heated so hot that sparks flew from them as from a furnace heated to the utmost, and their bodies were so scorched that all the people that stood by were savoured of the frying.

The iron chair had a long history. Ferdinand VII, King of Naples (1810–59), fought many military campaigns which led to the frequent capture of prisoners of war. For the interrogation of these prisoners, he ordered the construction of a specially designed portable chair, which could be folded and carried on the back of a mule. The ends of its legs were pointed, so that it could be fixed in the ground, and beneath its seat was a pan to hold burning charcoal.

Other instruments of torture and punishment

A wide variety of other inhuman devices have been used, principally as instruments of punishment, rather than to extract confession by torture. One of the most infamous of these was the 'ducking stool'. In its simplest form, a chair or stool was fixed to one end of a long pole, which was either pivoted on a support, or manhandled by a number of people. Sometimes it was mounted on a wheeled trolley, when it was known as a *trebuchet*, or 'treebucket', after the catapult of medieval warfare. A variation was the tumbril, or scolding cart. It had two wheels and shafts about 4.5m (15ft) long, by which it was pushed. One of these tumbrils, with the date 1686 carved on its wooden frame, existed formerly at Wootton Bassett in Wiltshire.

The victim was strapped in the seat, and then lowered into water, generally a muddy or stinking pond. The process could be repeated several times, until the victim, spluttering furiously, was nearly drowned – and, on at least one occasion, the outcome was death. The punishment was decreed for scolds and strumpets, and was popular in both England and Scotland.

The ducking stool in operation. The victim was strapped into a seat at one end of a long pole, and repeatedly lowered into the water.

Records of the use of the ducking stool in England cover more than two centuries. In 1534, two women of Sandwich, Kent, were expelled from the town for immoral acts, and warned that they would suffer the ducking stool, or the stocks, if they returned. At Wakefield, Yorkshire, in 1671:

> Foreasmuch as Jane, wife of William Farrett, shoemaker, stands indicted for a common scold, to the great annoyance and disturbance of her neighbours. It is therefore ordered that she should be openly ducked, and ducked three times over the head and ears by the constables of Selby, for which this call be their warrant.

The victim was strapped in the seat, and then lowered into water, generally a muddy or stinking pond

A visitor to Derby in the eighteenth century wrote: 'There is a curious and very useful machine, viz. a ducking stool, here for the benefit of scolding wives. A plan of this instrument I shall procure and transplant to Berkshire for the good of my native county.' And the parish records of Southam in Warwickshire, in 1718, detail the costs of making one. A man who had to visit Daventry to make a drawing of a stool was paid 3s 2d; the carpenter, the painter, and the blacksmith made their appropriate charges; and 9s 6d had to be paid to make the village pond sufficiently deep.

On 27 April 1745, the *London Evening Post* reported that 'a woman who keeps the Queen's Head alehouse at Kingston was ordered by the court to be ducked for scolding, and was accordingly placed in the chair and ducked in the Thames in the presence of two or three thousand people'.

The last recorded case in England was at Leominster, Herefordshire, in 1809. Jenny Pipes, alias Jane Corran, was paraded through the streets on a ducking stool mounted on a trolley. The centre post was 90cm (3ft) high, and the beam 8m (26ft) long. In 1817 a fellow-townswoman, Sarah Leeke, was sentenced to the same punishment, but, when the procession reached the edge of the river, the level of the water was found to be too low.

An unusual use of the ducking stool was reported by John Howard, in the second edition of *The State of the Prisons in England and Wales*, when he visited Liverpool Bridewell in 1779:

> In the courtyard is a pump, to which the women prisoners are tied every week and receive discipline. There is also a bath, with a new and singular contrivance. At one end of it was a standard for a long pole, at the extremity of which was fastened a chair. In this all the females … at their entrance, after a few questions, were placed, with a flannel shift on, and underwent a thorough ducking, thrice repeated – a use of a bath, which I dare say the legislature never thought of, when they ordered baths with a view to cleanliness and preserving the health of prisoners, and not for the exercise of a wanton and dangerous kind of severity.

The ducking stool certainly travelled from England to America. In 1818, it is recorded that one Mary Davis was publicly ducked for scolding. And in 1889 a Mrs Mary Brady was charged in Jersey City with being a 'common scold'. As Geoffrey Abbott, a former yeoman warder in the Tower of London, has put it: 'On referring to their law books, incredulous lawyers found that scolding was still an indictable offence in New Jersey, and the ducking stool was still available for use, as it was not abolished when new statutes were adopted'.

Another common punishment for women was the 'scold's bridle', or 'branks', described in George Riley Scott's *A History of Torture* (1940):

> This bridle was constructed of iron, something after the fashion of a helmet, except that it was merely a framework, and offered no obstruction to the sight, or the movement of anything other than the tongue, which was effectively silenced by a piece of iron, which projected into the mouth, acting as a gag; and, it may be stated, an exceedingly uncomfortable and cruel gag at that ... The specimens which have been preserved in many museums throughout the kingdom indicate the variety of designs that were used, some of which were undoubtedly capable of inflicting severe pain and injury, and the wearing of which, even for a short time, must have constituted a form of torture. In some cases the part which penetrated the mouth was sharply rowelled like a spur, or studded with spikes.

In Scotland, in particular, the bridle was also used in the punishment of witches, as in the case of Agnes Sampson, one of the North Berwick witches (see Chapter 7, page 119). It was believed that witches were able to turn themselves into animals and transport themselves through space, as they wished. The bridle was specifically intended to prevent this.

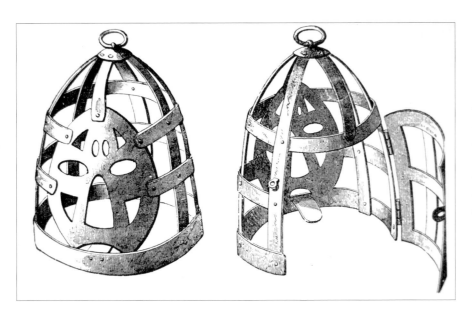

The 'scold's bridle', or 'branks'. The projecting iron gag can be seen clearly in the right-hand illustration. Sometimes this was sharpened like a spur, or (as in this case) studded with small spikes.

A less severe punishment, used principally in Scotland for offences such as failing to attend divine service, was the 'jougs', also known as the 'bregan', or 'bradyeane'. This was an iron collar that was locked about the culprit's neck, with a chain that could be attached to the porch of the church or chapel, or to the town's market cross. Henry Machyn noted in his *Diary*:

> The 30th day of June, 1553, was set a post hard by the Standard in Cheap, and a young fellow tied to the post with a collar of iron about his neck, and another to the post with a chain, and two men whipping them about the post, for pretended visions and opprobrious and seditious words.

Although intended as a temporary punishment, sentencing to the jougs could sometimes have more serious consequences. In 1541 in London, one John Porter was charged with the crime of reading the Bible, carried to Newgate, and locked in the jougs. He was later found dead; it seems he had fainted, and strangled in the collar.

A very unusual form of torture, of which only a single account has survived, was practised upon Juan van Halen by the Spanish Inquisition in Murcia. In September 1817 he was charged with a political offence, which he steadfastly denied. In prison, two high crutches were placed under his armpits, so that his feet were off the floor. His right arm was bound to one crutch, and his body and legs to both, while his left hand was put into a tightly fitting wooden glove, with two iron rods extending to his shoulder to keep it in a horizontal position:

> The glove which guided my arm, and which seemed to be resting on the edge of a wheel, began now to turn, and with its movements I felt by degrees an acute pain, especially from the elbow to the shoulder, a general convulsion throughout my frame, and a cold sweat overspreading my face. The interrogatory continued; but Zorilla's question of 'Is it so? Is it so?' were the only words that struck my ear amidst the excruciating pain I endured, which became so intense that I fainted away, and heard no more the voices of those cannibals.

A History of the Inquisition, 1850

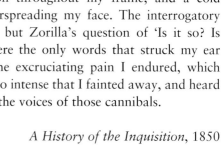

An example of the Scottish 'jougs', from Forfar. Intended as a relatively mild form of punishment, it could at times prove fatal, if the victim collapsed and strangled in the collar.

The treadmill and the crank

Torture might have been abolished in England, and such punishments as the ducking stool and the scold's bridle fallen into disuse, but during the nineteenth century the prison authorities made use of other torments. One of these was the treadmill, which was described by Henry Mayhew in *The Criminal Prisons of London* (1862):

> The machine was the brainchild of a Mr Cubitt, an engineer from Lowestoft in Suffolk. This gentleman, on visiting Bury St Edmunds gaol with a magistrate, remarked upon the large number of prisoners seen lounging idly about in groups, the whole aspect indicating a demoralizing waste of time and energy. 'I wish to God, Mr Cubitt,' said the justice, 'you could suggest to us some mode of employing those fellows. Could nothing like a wheel become available?'
>
> An instantaneous idea flashed through the mind of Mr Cubitt. And Cubitt whispered to himself, 'The wheel elongated!'. And merely saying to his interrogator 'Something has struck me which may prove worthy of further consideration, and perhaps you will hear from me upon the subject', he took his leave. After giving it due thought, he was able to fashion all the mechanical requirements into practical form, and so invented the Treadwheel, surely the most pointless machine ever devised, yet one which was adopted by prisons throughout the country, and used to occupy the time of their inmates.

John Porter was charged with the crime of reading the Bible and locked in the jougs.

William Cubitt, who was knighted in 1851, had already invented a device for the automatic regulation of windmills' sails; later he constructed the Oxford and Liverpool Junction canals, the South Eastern Railway, and the Berlin waterworks, and became President of the Institution of Civil Engineers. The treadmill, by contrast, did nothing useful.

Cubitt's invention was first installed in Brixton prison, London, in 1817. It was a great wheel, like a waterwheel but very wide, with treads that could accommodate between 10 and 40 prisoners, standing shoulder to shoulder. Prisoners were able to grasp a succession of rungs above their heads, as they stepped upward from tread to tread. As the row of prisoners was forced to step forward in unison, the wheel revolved, and anyone who missed their footing, or attempted to move with a rhythm different from the others, would find himself flung round inside the wheel.

The effort was equivalent to climbing an endless flight of steps, and a quarter of an hour's labour on the wheel was sufficient to exhaust even the fittest. At the end of those 15 minutes, a bell would ring, and a second shift of prisoners would replace the first. But, after 15 minutes rest, the first shift would again be consigned to the wheel, and, in all, each shift would complete some 15 periods each day.

Although the authorities offered the treadmill as a source of power for industry, there were no takers. Instead, the wheel was used to drive a giant windmill in the prison yard; this was fitted with sails that could be adjusted to increase the resistance of the machine. Not for nothing was this known as 'grinding the wind'.

This form of hard labour was commonly employed in English prisons for about 25 years. It was succeeded by the 'crank'. In one form this was an iron drum, standing on legs, with a cranked handle protruding from one side. Inside, the handle turned an axle on which a succession of scoops was mounted; these picked up sand from the bottom of the drum, which was emptied out again as the axle revolved.

A dial on the front registered the number of revolutions of the crank, and the prisoner was required to turn the handle 10,000 times in the course of a day. A committee (1852–3) appointed to inquire into the conditions in a Birmingham prison, reported:

We were assured that, in order to accomplish such a task, a boy would necessarily exert a force equal to one fourth of the ordinary work of a draught horse; the average estimate of the work of a boy, in ordinary labour out of a prison, being about one tenth of the same; and, indeed, that no human being, whether adult or juvenile, could continue to perform such an amount of labour of this kind for

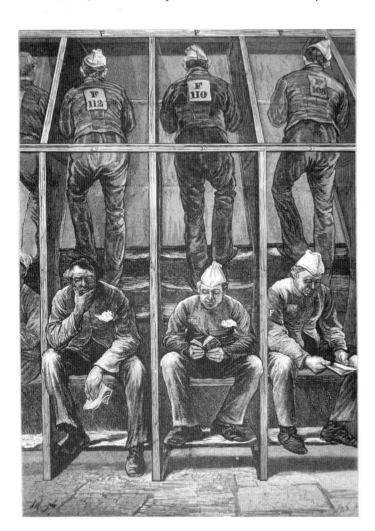

The treadmill in the Clerkenwell House of Correction, London, in 1874. The front row of convicts are resting at the end of their 15-minute shift.

several consecutive days, especially on a prison diet, without wasting much and suffering greatly.

The committee was told of the case of Edward Andrews, aged 15, who was sentenced to three months imprisonment for stealing 4lb (1.8kg) of beef. He was put to the crank and, failing to achieve the required number of revolutions, was given only bread and water. A few days later, he again was unsuccessful, and punishment was meted out in the same way.

On the third occasion he broke the machine dial – whether deliberately, by accident, or by trying too hard is not recorded – and was put in the 'punishment jacket'. This was a kind of strait-jacket, with a high, rigid leather collar, so tight that a boy 'could not bite a piece of bread held to his mouth'; in this, the prisoner was strapped to the wall in a standing position for hours at a time.

For the length of a month, Andrews endured a succession of these punishments. Then he was found by the nightwatchman, hanging dead by his hammock strap from one of the bars of his cell window.

'After giving it due thought, he invented the Treadwheel, surely the most pointless machine ever devised'

Electrical equipment

The use of electricity is the signal contribution of the twentieth century to torture. In the earliest days, it was sufficient to connect the victim to the terminals of an army signals magneto – the *gégène* described in Chapter 11 (page 169) – or even to the public mains supply, an operation dangerous to both victim and torturer. Magnetos discovered in Turkish police stations have been said to be specially manufactured for this purpose. A victim of police brutality in Turkey in 1972 reported:

> They attached wires to my fingers and toes, and passed electric current through my body … After a while, they disconnected the wire from my finger and connected it to my ear. They immediately gave a high dose of electricity. My whole body and head shook in a terrible way. My front teeth started breaking. At the same time my torturers would hold a mirror to my face and say: 'Look what is happening to your lovely green eyes. Soon you will not be able to see at all. You will lose your mind. See, you have already started bleeding in your mouth.'
>
> *A Glimpse of Hell*, Amnesty International, 1996

Equipment specifically developed for electric shock treatment was the 'Apollo' machine, used by the secret police of the Shah of Iran,

'My whole body and head shook in a terrible way. My front teeth started breaking.'

and by the religious police of the succeeding regime. While it delivered shocks to sensitive parts of the body, it also incorporated a steel helmet that covered the head and amplified the victim's screams.

Technology has now produced a more efficient apparatus, which has been described as 'the most universal modern tool of the torturers': the 'electroshock baton', a development of a simple piece of farmer's equipment, the cattle prod. The modern pulsed-discharge baton is said to be up to 100 times more powerful. According to the manufacturer, 'biomedical research' was the basis of its development during the 1980s.

The British Forensic Science Service was commissioned by the Home Office to investigate the effects of these electroshock devices. Their report stated that a typical discharge of up to half a second would startle and repel the victim; after contact of between one and two seconds, the victim was unable to remain standing; three to five seconds would result in complete loss of skeletal muscle control. The effects of the shock can persist for between 5 and 15 minutes.

Allegedly intended only for crowd control, the electroshock baton is also a powerful instrument of torture. It is most often applied to the genitals, nipples, or lips (the most sensitive parts of the body), but also to the fingers, toes, or earlobes. In China this is known as *dian ji*. In Lhasa, Tibet, in 1987, a 13-year-old boy had electric shocks applied to his torso, and an electric baton was then put into his mouth. He was later released without charges.

Portable electrified riot shields are also available. These are made of transparent polycarbonate, in which metal strips are embedded. A button-operated induction coil in the handle charges up a capacitator, which then discharges, producing bright violet sparks and a frightening crackle. Between 40,000 and 100,000 volts can be produced. A sales video made by the manufacturer shows how the victim is instantly thrown to the ground, unable to move.

A further development is a belt that will deliver an electric shock by remote control. Known as 'remote control electronically activated custody technology (REACT)', it is made by Stuntech Inc of Cleveland, Ohio. The company's sales literature asks: 'After all, if you were wearing a contraption around your waist, that by the mere push of a button in someone else's hand, could make you defecate or urinate yourself, what would that do to you from the psychological standpoint?'

Although it is primarily designed for the control of prison inmates, there is obviously a potential for this as a device of deliberate torture. And no doubt other equally ingenious devices are being conceived. 'Man's inhumanity to Man' knows no bounds.

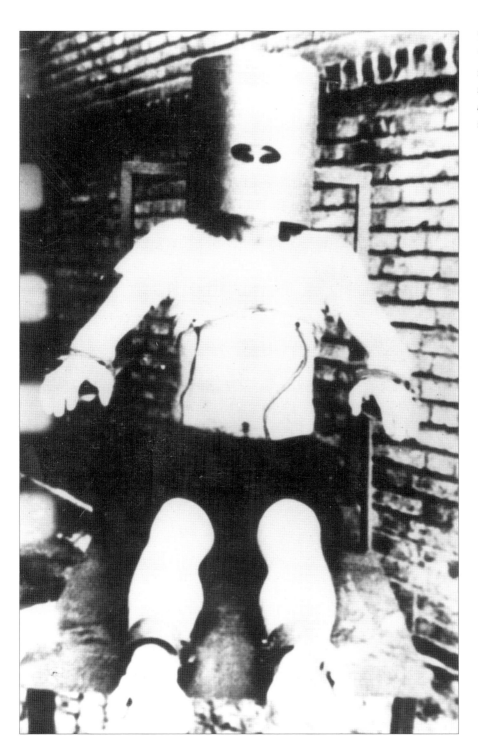

The electric shock 'Apollo machine', reportedly still in use in Iran. The helmet amplifies the victim's screams.

Chapter Nine

China, Japan & India

Long before the twentieth century, China had the reputation of being the country in which torture took more bizarre and ingenious forms, and was practised with greater cruelty, than anywhere else in the world. However, as George Riley Scott wrote in *A History of Torture* (1940):

> Much of this reputation is due to the description, in books of fiction, of forms of torture which have originated largely in the fertile imagination of sensational novelists … As regards those tortures authorized by the Chinese authorities … it is doubtful if they exceeded, either in their elements of the bizarre or in their brutality, the methods adopted for similar purposes in many reputedly more civilized countries.

The Chinese equivalents of the 'Spanish boot' and the thumbscrews, used in the interrogation of unwilling witnesses or to force a confession from criminals, were described by the Portuguese F. Alvarez Semedo in his *History of China*, published in London in 1655:

> For the feet they use an instrument called *kia quen*. It consisteth of three pieces of wood put in one traverse, that in the middle is fixt, the other two are moveable, between these the feet are put, where they are squeezed and prest, till the heel-bone run into the foot: for the hands they use also certain small pieces of wood between the fingers, they call them *tean zu*, then they straiten them very hard, and seale them round about with paper, and so they leave them for some space of time.

The use of these instruments was also described in 1810 by Sir George Staunton, in his *Penal Code of China*. According to Staunton, the torture was used particularly in cases of robbery or homicide, and if the first operation did not result in a confession it was lawful to repeat it a second time. However, it could not be used on suspected criminals under the age of 15 or older than 70, nor on the diseased or crippled. The *kia quen* was usually reserved for male criminals, and the *tean zu* for females.

(Opposite) The terrible Chinese ling chi, *'death by a thousand cuts'. The prisoner was fastened to a crude cross of wood, and the executioner progressively cut handfuls of flesh from the thighs and breast, and then from the joints. Next, the nose, ears, toes, and fingers were cut off, followed by the limbs, in stages. Finally the victim was stabbed in the heart, and his head cut off.*

If these methods failed to elicit the necessary information, the torturer would use a bastinado made of bamboo. The victim was beaten rhythmically, and with quite gentle blows, on the soles of the feet. This apparently lightweight treatment, continued for any length of time, would relatively quickly produce a state of hysteria in the victim. Sometimes the bare buttocks, rather than the feet, were beaten. Alternatively, in more severe interrogations, a piece of split bamboo would be used: the edges of the fibres, as sharp as a scalpel, would lacerate the flesh at every stroke. According to Semedo's account, 'they do many times die of the bastinadoes they receive'.

Under the Manchu dynasty, which ruled China from the seventeenth century until 1912, the torturers practised on blocks of bean curd until they became so expert with the bastinado that they could strike hundreds of times without drawing blood, or, if required, lacerate the flesh with a couple of blows.

Sir Henry Norman witnessed punishment with the bastinado upon the buttocks, and described it in his book *The People and Politics of the Far East* (1895):

A torturer using the bastinado. This was made of bamboo, and the victim was struck lightly, but rhythmically, on the bare flesh of the soles of the feet, or the buttocks. Torturers became so expert that they could strike hundreds of times without drawing blood.

After a few more minutes of the dactylic rap-tap-tap, rap-tap-tap, a deep groan broke from the prisoner's lips. I walked over to look at him, and saw that his face was blue … Then it became congested with blood, and whereas at first he had lain quiet of his own accord, now a dozen men were holding him tight.

Sir Henry also described another form of torture, the name of which he translated from the Chinese as 'kneeling on chains'. This was exactly what it was. Victims were lowered face-downward by a rope attached to their thumbs and big toes, so that the whole of their weight rested on a coil of chain, the links of which had razor-sharp edges. This was generally sufficient to secure a confession of guilt from a suspected criminal.

For less serious offences, the Chinese employed a form of punishment similar to the European pillory, variously known as the cangue, *tcha*, or *kea*. Semedo describes it as 'the punishment of *kian hao*':

> It is a great thick board, four or five palmes square, with a hole cut in the middle of it about the bigness of a man's neck. This they fasten about their necks, and to it are hung two scrolls of paper of a hand's breadth, wherein are written his fault, and the cause of his punishment; they serve also to show that the board has not been opened; and so with these great boards about their necks, these poor wretches are ... exposed to shame in the public streets, for 15, 20, or 30 days, according as they are adjudged by their sentence, whose greatest rigor is that during all that time these boards are not taken off their necks, neither night nor day.

This punishment is referred to in the *I Ching*, a Chinese oracle text more than 3000 years old:

> *Shih hoh*: Biting through:
> His neck is locked in the wooden cangue;
> His ears are gone.
> Great misfortune.

Since the cangue made it impossible for the victim to reach his hands to his mouth, he was likely to die from lack of food and drink without the assistance of relatives or friends.

More severe than the cangue was the punishment reserved for a monk found guilty of fornication. According to B. Picart, in his book *Religious Ceremonies* (1737), the culprit had a hole bored through his neck with a hot iron, through which was threaded a long chain. Then, stripped to his undershirt or even naked, he was led begging through the streets by another monk; every time he tried to ease the agony by lifting the weight of the chain with his hands, the second monk would whip him. This punishment continued until the culprit had collected sufficient alms for his monastery to absolve his sin.

When the verdict was death, the Chinese generally employed strangulation or decapitation, but the most famous – and most horrific – of all the Chinese methods of capital punishment was the *ling chi*, or 'death by a thousand cuts'. The sadism of this protracted form of execution was sometimes compounded by an element of chance. The executioner would bring in a cloth-covered basket containing an assortment of knives, each marked with a part of the body. He would

The culprit had a hole bored through his neck with a hot iron

Even in the 20th century, Chinese criminals had to suffer the punishment of the cangue, a thick board that locked round the neck. They were then paraded daily in the streets. As the boards were not removed for as much as a month, they were unable to feed themselves, and had to rely upon the sympathy of others.

take out a knife at random, and slash at the part of the body named on the handle. It was said that the relatives of the condemned would bribe the executioner to bring out the knife labelled 'heart', in order to end the victim's ordeal as swiftly as possible.

However, the executioner frequently used only a single knife, slowly dismembering his victim step by step. Sir Henry Norman described such a process. The criminal was fastened to a crude cross of wood, and the executioner progressively cut pieces 'from the fleshy parts of the body, such as the thighs and breast'. Next, 'the joints and excrescences of the body' were gradually sliced away, followed by the nose, ears, toes, and fingers. 'Then the limbs are cut off piecemeal at the wrists and ankles, the elbows and the knees, the shoulders and the hips. Finally, the victim is stabbed to the heart, and his head cut off.'

Japan

The Japanese are also notorious for their obsession with cruelty. For centuries the judicial courts of Japan accepted torture as a legitimate way of obtaining information from both suspected criminals and witnesses reluctant to give evidence. In 1926 Joseph Longford edited and revised James Murdoch's *History of Japan*, in which four different forms of torture were described. The most common was flogging, on the thighs and buttocks, with a special cane made of three strips of split bamboo bound together, with up to 150 strokes being given. Judicial torture was officially abolished in 1873, but Longford wrote:

> ... the present writer had every reason to believe that torture was still, and not rarely, used in local police offices, while it is notorious that it was freely used with pristine severity on alleged rebels, both in Korea and Formosa, often on persons who were entirely innocent. I knew, from unquestionable authority, of many instances in Formosa.

And the unfortunate Allied prisoners of the Japanese during World War II could certainly bring more recent evidence.

The second form of torture was known as 'hugging the stone'. Heavy weights of stone were piled on prisoners' thighs while they knelt on a pile of knife-edged flints. In the third form, victims were bound extremely tightly by their arms and legs, and kept in this posture until they showed signs of approaching death. In the fourth, the arms were strapped behind the back with rope around the wrists, and the victims were hung from a hook; due to the weight, the rope gradually cut through the flesh of their wrists to the bone.

During the seventeenth century, the Tokugawa regime made strenuous efforts to drive Christianity out of Japan, employing similar methods to those of the Inquisition in combating heresy. Men, women, and even the children of those who professed Christian beliefs were thrown naked into the rivers. Strapped on the backs of horses, they were driven through the town streets while boiling water was flung at them. Some were boiled alive in hot volcanic springs. In September 1622, at Nagasaki, 50 Christians were burned alive. Others were tied by their four limbs, each to the leg of an ox, and so torn in pieces.

The Dutch writers Francis Caron and Joost Schorten provided a horrifying account, which was translated in 1671 as *A True Description of the Mighty Kingdoms of Japan and Siam*:

> They forced the women and more tender maids to go upon their hands and feet, bowing, supporting and dragging them naked in the presence of thousands through the streets; that done, they caused them to be ravished and lain with by Russians and villains, and then throwing them, so stript and abused, into great deep tubs full of snakes and adders, which crept by several passages into their bodies, suffered them to perish unspeakable miseries in their fearful manner.
>
> They thrust hurds into the mothers' privities, and binding the sons about with the same combustible matter, thrust and forced them, as

'the joints and excrescences of the body' were gradually sliced away

also the fathers and daughters, to set fire to each other, whereby they underwent unconceivable torments and pains; some they clothed with sods, and poured hot scalding water continually upon them, tortured them in that manner till they died, which dured two or three daies ... hundreds of them being stript naked, and burnt in the foreheads that they might be known, and driven into the woods and forests, all men being commanded by proclamation, upon pain of death, not to assist them with either meat, drink, clothing or lodging; many more put into pinfolds upon the sea-shore, and kept there half their time dry and half wet, being every tide overflown by the sea; but these were permitted to eat and drink, to keep them longer alive in their misery, which lasted ordinarily ten or twelve daies. ...

At last they found a more hellish and exquisite way of torturing than before: they hung these sufferers by the heels, their heads in pits, which to give the blood some vent, they slash lightly crossways (but they do that now no more) and in this posture they live several daies, ten or twelve, and speak sensibly to the very last ... This extremity hath indeed (by reason of its continuance) forced many to renounce their religion; and some of them who hung two or three daies, assured me that the pains they endured were wholly unsufferable, no fire nor no torture equalling their languor and violence.

The Japanese torture known as 'hugging the stone'. Heavy blocks of stone were piled on the prisoner's thighs while he knelt on a board studded with sharp flints.

When it came to criminal execution, the Japanese were as ingenious as the Chinese. There was the 'execution of twenty-one cuts' – which may, in a way, be considered more merciful than the 'thousand cuts' inflicted in China. Eyewitnesses described the death of a rebel chieftain:

> With superhuman command of self, the unhappy Mowung bore silently the slow and deliberate slicing-off – first of his cheeks, then of his breasts, the muscles of upper and lower arms, the calves of his legs, etc, etc, care being taken throughout to avoid touching any immediately vital part. Once only he murmured an entreaty that he might be killed outright – a request, of course, unheeded by men who took a savage pleasure in skilfully torturing their victim.

Once only he murmured an entreaty that he might be killed outright

India

In India, a wide variety of psychological as well as physical tortures were employed. In his *Oriental Memoirs* (1813), James Forbes describes a typical case in which both approaches were combined:

> The collector of customs was a Hindoo of family, wealth and credit. Lulled into security from his interest at court, and so suspecting no evil, he was surprised by a visit from the vizier, with a company of armed men, to demand his money; which being secreted, no threatenings could induce him to discover. A variety of tortures were inflicted to extort a confession; one was a sofa, with a platform of tight cordage in network, covered with a chintz palampore, which concealed a bed of thorns placed under it: the collector, a corpulent banian, was then stripped of his jama, or muslin robe, and ordered to lie down on the couch: the cords bending with his weight, sunk on the bed of thorns; these long and piercing thorns of the baubul or forest acacia, which being placed purposely with their points upwards, lacerated the wretched man, whether in motion or at rest. For two days and nights he bore the torture without revealing the secret; his tormentors fearing he would die before their purpose was effected, had recourse to another mode of compulsion. When nature was nearly exhausted, they took him from the bed, and supported him on the floor, until his infant son, an only child, was brought into the room; and with him a bag containing a fierce cat, into which they put the child, and tied up the mouth of the sack. The agents of cruelty stood over them with bamboos, ready at a signal to beat the bag, and enrage the cat to destroy the child: this was too much for a father's heart! he produced his treasure.

The chief torturer and executioner of a district in India, photographed in the 1890s.

This was very likely a case of the biter bitten, for revenue officials frequently used torture to extract quite minor sums. A favourite method was known as *anundal*. It required no equipment other than a length of rope, with which the torturer exercised his ingenuity in tying his victim into the most unnatural positions:

The head of the prisoner would be forced down and tied to his feet by means of a rope or belt passed around his neck and under his toes. Or one leg would be forced upwards to the uttermost extent and fastened to the neck, compelling the victim to stand in this agonizing position. Or the arms and legs, forcibly interlaced to the point almost of dislocation, were bound so as to be immovable. In other cases heavy stones were fastened to the victim's back, which was often stripped naked, the sharp edges cutting into the flesh. ... and in almost every case the torture was practised under the powerful rays of the Indian sun.

A History of Torture,
George Riley Scott, 1940

A report of an investigation in 1855 into torture in Madras includes a description of what happened to Vencatachela Rajaulee and his father. To compel them to pay a sum of 10 rupees, they were 'placed in *anundal*, their legs tied together, and their heads tied to their feet in a stooping posture; their hands were tied behind them, and stones placed upon their backs; in which posture they were made to stand from six in the morning until noon. It will hardly be a matter of surprise that the father died the following month.'

Torturers often exploited the hot Indian climate. Sometimes culprits were made to run up and down in the prison compound for hours, or chained to a cart and forced to follow it for long distances. Or they were sewn up inside the hide of a newly skinned buffalo or sheep, and exposed to the sun; as the hide dried, it shrank, gradually squeezing the flesh from the unfortunate victims, until they died in agony.

Other torments included tying prisoners to trees, with their faces smeared with honey to attract red ants; or putting a biting insect, such as a carpenter beetle, into a small cage that was then strapped to a sensitive part of the body.

Few specific instruments of torture were thought necessary when human ingenuity could devise such simple methods as those described above. One exception was the *kittee*, which consisted of two hinged wooden plates, and which was used in much the same way as the thumbscrews in Europe, or the Chinese *kia quen*. It could be applied to various small and sensitive parts of the body. There was also a larger version that could be used to squeeze the hands or feet.

In a variation of the *kittee*, victims were laid on their backs across a thick bamboo rod, while a second rod was placed across the chest; two strong men then exerted heavy pressure at each end of the upper rod.

One case of torture peculiar to India involved a certain Subapatha Pillay. He was tied by the legs and hung upside down, while chilli powder was forced up his nose. A strong belt was gradually tightened around his waist, and the result, according to the report of this case, was 'too revoltingly indecent to be referred to'.

There was also a method of execution that was particular to India – being tortured and trampled to death by an elephant. A description was published in *The Percy Anecdotes* of 1823:

> The criminal was placed three yards [two and a half metres] behind on the ground, his legs tied by three ropes, which were fastened to a ring on the hind leg of the animal. At every step the elephant took, it jerked him forwards, and eight or ten steps must have dislocated every limb, for they were loose and broken when the elephant had proceeded 500 yards [450 metres]. The man, though covered with mud, showed every sign of life, and seemed to be in the most excruciating torments. After ... about an hour, he was taken to the outside of the town, when the elephant, which is instructed for such purposes, is backed, and puts his foot on the head of the criminal.

Other torments included tying prisoners to trees, with their faces smeared with honey to attract red ants

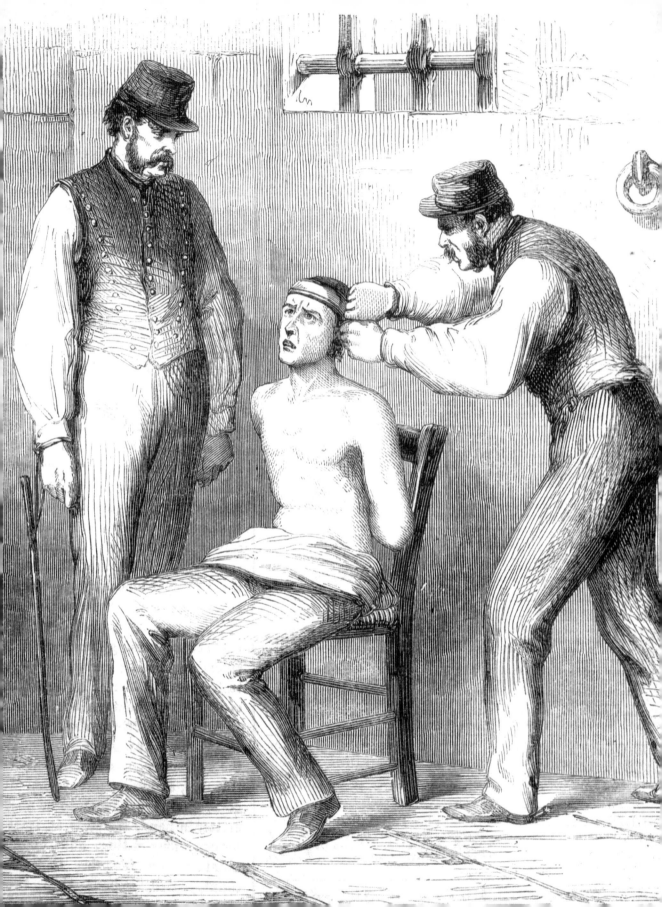

Chapter Ten

Suppressing the Opposition

Despite all the fine words spoken by humanitarians, and despite its legal abolition at the end of the eighteenth century by most countries who considered themselves to be civilized, the practice of torture, in its varied forms, continued in many parts of the world. And nowhere was the brutality more widespread, and more infamous, than in British India.

The sadistic practices of the Indian tax gatherers have already been described (see Chapter 9, page 153), but torture reigned at all levels of Indian society under the administration of the East India Company. In 1846 a certain Mr Theobald – 'an English gentleman of high standing at the Calcutta bar' – was robbed of a bag containing 400 rupees while travelling to Barrackpore in Bengal. The thief was arrested within an hour, and to Theobald's horror, the local *darogah* (chief of police) offered to torture him.

Theobald had contacts in London, notably among members of the India Reform Society, who were strongly opposed to the East India Company's monopolistic control of India. The governor of Bengal refused to allow any inquiry into the use of torture, but in 1854 the Society was able to set up a commission in Madras.

This commission sat for seven months, during which time it heard evidence from people throughout Madras. So keen, in fact, was one witness to appear before it that he actually walked 1600km (1000 miles). The commission found that torture was widely used, and not only in tax gathering or obtaining confessions from criminals; it was also employed by the *darogahs* to enrich themselves by extortion. The most usual means of torture was *kittee*, or *anundal* (see Chapter 9, pages 154–5), but others included:

... twisting rope round the arm to impede circulation; lifting up by the moustache; suspending by the arms tied behind the back; searing with hot irons; placing scratching insects, such as the carpenter beetle, in the navel, scrotum and other sensitive parts; dipping in wells and rivers until the party is half-suffocated; beating with sticks; prevention of sleep;

(Opposite) Torture of a political prisoner in Sicily, 1860. A rope about the victim's forehead is steadily tightened by twisting, producing intense pain.

nipping the flesh with pincers; putting peppers and red chillies in the eyes, or introducing them into the private parts of men and women ...

The efforts of the reformers might have borne fruit sooner if they had had not been overtaken by events, with the outbreak of the Indian Mutiny (which brought the rule of the East India Company to an end) in 1857. It was not until 1871 that the Indian Evidence Act introduced specific rules that were designed to prevent the obtaining of confessions by coercion, but the allegations of torture continued – and even increased in number.

Even in 1908, nearly 40 years later, a court in the Punjab sentenced a woman, Gulab Bano, to death when she confessed to poisoning her husband. Her appeal against the sentence was upheld when a civil surgeon gave evidence to confirm her account of being hung upside down from the roof of the local police station, while a baton smeared with chillies was thrust into her anus.

Allegations of torture were disposed of by the simple expedient of suppressing the newspapers

But the Indian government consistently supported the police, because there were matters more serious than individual crimes to be dealt with. Kaiser Wilhelm of Germany had his eyes on India: the Germans were building a railway across Persia toward the frontier, and encouraging nationalist terrorists in the subcontinent itself. British officials were murdered, and in 1908, in Calcutta, two Englishwomen were killed by a bomb thrown into their carriage in the mistaken belief that it was the carriage of the chief magistrate.

Over the next five years, hundreds of young men were arrested and charged with 'conspiracy to wage war against the King-Emperor [George V]'. Although many confessed, it emerged that their confessions had been illegally obtained by the police. The nationalist newspapers alleged that torture had been used, and it was established that – at the very least – the prisoners had been beaten and stoned, deprived of sleep, subjected to solitary confinement, and threatened that action would be taken against their parents.

The allegations of torture were disposed of by the simple expedient of suppressing the newspapers that made them. The Indian government then took the view that as few complaints were made, there was little evidence of torture. It pointed out that confessions were in fact frequently corroborated by the recovery of stolen goods, or other material evidence:

The obtaining of the confession is not the sole, or even the principal motive which induces incompetent or dishonest police officers to resort to a mixture of threatening, coaxing, worry, or ill-usage; their object is rather to induce the accused to give up the stolen property, or to indicate where some clue may be found ...

Mr Justice Beaman, a British judge, disagreed:

It is in my opinion safe to say that, excepting violent crimes ... all other confessions have been directly or indirectly induced by improper means ... Where actual torture is not used, the knowledge that it will be used may induce a number of criminals, who would not otherwise confess, to do so in anticipation of the methods they dread being employed on them.

With the outbreak of World War I in 1914, the government was able to introduce emergency measures, and several hundred terrorist suspects were interned. But the Russian revolution of 1917 raised the authorities' fears once more, and a series of laws – the so-called Rowlatt Acts – provided for measures to be taken in the face of 'revolutionary or anarchical crime'. Mahatma Gandhi denounced them as 'unjust, subversive to the principles of liberty and justice, and destructive of the elementary rights of individuals'.

In the years that followed, hundreds of thousands (many of them innocent of any crime) were imprisoned. Gandhi wrote to the Viceroy:

The execution of two sepoys, found guilty during the Indian Mutiny of 1857. The mutiny set back the efforts of those concerned with the suppression of torture in India by many years.

Whilst known leaders have been dealt with more or less according to legal formality, the rank and file have been often savagely, ... even indecently assaulted ... Accounts have come to me from Bengal, Bihar, Uthal, United Provinces, Delhi and Bombay confirming the experiences of Gujerat ... Bones have been broken, private parts have been squeezed ...

The Indian leader Mahatma Ghandi denounced the torture of his followers by the authorities, during the 1920s.

Even in the 1940s, nationalist pamphlets were accusing the police of torture 'by the strappado, the application of chilli powder to the genitals of men and women, and anal penetration with a variety of instruments'. Lester Hutchinson, one of three Englishmen accused in a communist conspiracy, described prison conditions in his book, *Conspiracy at Meerut*:

The warders, and even the convict-overseers, entertain themselves through the long hours by striking and torturing prisoners, and the jailer often holds what is known as a 'blanket parade'. The prisoner against whom the jailer has a grievance is placed flat on the ground and covered with blankets; he is then beaten through the blankets with bamboo rods wielded by the jailers' trustworthy minions, so that although he receives all the pain of the beating he has no wounds to show the superintendent to justify his complaint, and, indeed, it is not wise to complain; for complaints do not lead to rectification of evils, but to further punishment and torture.

The legacy of British rule survived the achievement of Indian independence. When Mrs Indira Gandhi declared a state of emergency in June 1975, claimed Dr Subramanyam

Swamy, the leader of the Janata party, 'the police made people drink their own urine, ducked them in ice-cold water, administered electric shocks, denied water and food continuously for days together …'.

Revolutionaries in Europe

Fear of revolution brought about a revival of torture during the nineteenth century both in colonial administrations and in Europe. In 1851 William Ewart Gladstone, the future British prime minister, paid a private visit to Naples. At that time Italy was a divided country. In the north, the various Italian states were contested between the Austrians and the French; the centre was controlled by the Vatican; and in the south were the twin kingdoms of Naples and Sicily. There was a widespread desire for the political unification of the country: in 1848 Milan, Piedmont, and Sardinia declared war on Austria, while Sicily revolted against Neapolitan rule. The condition of the revolutionary prisoners in the dungeons of Naples and Cefalu aroused Mr Gladstone's wrath, and resulted in the publication of details in the British press.

Friends and relatives of Sicilian patriots had been tortured to reveal where they were hiding, principally by means of a type of thumbscrew, the *strumento angelico*. The victims of this instrument were even prevented from screaming by the *cuffia del silenzio*, a tight leather muzzle.

Torture did not occur only under Neapolitan rule. The Inquisition raised its head again in the Vatican states, and in the north the Austrians, who had abolished torture in the 1780s, reintroduced it. The revolutionary Felice Orsini described the scene in an Austrian prison in 1854 in his book, *The Austrian Dungeons in Italy* (tr. 1856):

> Passing from my cell to the examination hall, I often saw a poor victim stretched on the *cavaletto*, a bench about eight feet [two and a half metres] in length, with his face downwards. By means of a movable vice in the centre, the body is screwed down, so that the sufferer cannot stir, the arms are stretched above the head, and the wrists are fastened to irons at the ankle, so that the foot remains beyond the bench. A corporal … stands to the left of the victim, and commences administering the torture thus: holding a switch aloft in his right hand, he swings it across his victim, and up to the left, with as much force as he can muster, saying *ein*; returning to the right, he says *zwei*, and again to the left, *drei* … If the victim speaks, the flogging is suspended to note down his depositions. At the conclusion of the operation the surgeon examines him, and he is borne back to his bed of straw. If he has remained firm in his refusal to confess, the punishment is renewed on the following day.

Fear of revolution brought about a revival of torture during the nineteenth century

Chapter Eleven

Torture in the Twentieth Century

Despite the internationally accepted Geneva Conventions respecting the victims of war, the use of torture – particularly in wartime – has continued throughout most of the twentieth century. Its most notorious employment was during World War II (1939–45), both in Nazi Germany, and in Japanese prisoner-of-war camps.

By the time war was declared, the civil authorities in Germany already had considerable experience in the persecution of whole sections of their own society – Jews, gypsies, homosexuals, and political dissidents. Acutely conscious of those members of their own armed forces being held in prison camps, the Germans were generally meticulous in their treatment of Allied military prisoners. This meticulousness did not, however, extend to Resistance fighters or captured secret agents, who did not wear uniforms or carry service papers, were not protected by the Geneva Conventions, and who were regarded as spies. While it was internationally agreed that convicted spies could be executed out of hand, there was no justification for the use of torture in their interrogation. However, this was the role in which the Gestapo was to become infamous.

The German secret police, the *Geheimstaatspolizei*, was inaugurated in March 1932 at a meeting that included Ernst Röhm, chief of staff of the SA (Brown Shirts); Josef Goebbels; Hitler's deputy Rudolf Hess; and Heinrich Himmler, the leader of the SS (*Schutzstaffel* – protective force). The Gestapo had two responsibilities: the investigation of security inside Germany; and the interrogation of those involved in external subversion and espionage.

The Gestapo, as part of the 'Führer executive', was outside the law: 'to this machine were allotted all those political tasks in which Hitler was really interested; ...the preservation of his own power, demographic policy, the policy for the occupation of conquered territory, persecution of all actual and supposed opponents of the regime.'

(Opposite) The 'killing fields' of Cambodia, during the reign of Pol Pot (1975–9), saw the death of millions. Piles of the victims' skulls have been discovered.

The interrogation of Odette (Mrs Peter Churchill), a British agent arrested in Marseille in 1943, is a suitable example of Gestapo techniques. Held in Fresnes prison, in the south of Paris, Odette was taken one day to the Gestapo headquarters at 84 Avenue Foch, in the centre of the city. Her interrogator, looking 'as if he had just come out of a cold bath', smelt of eau-de-Cologne. When she refused to answer his questions, a second man came into the room, and held her arms behind the back of her chair. The interrogator came forward, and began to unbutton her blouse. Odette said sharply that she would do this herself.

One of her arms was released, and she undid the first few buttons. The second man pulled the back of the blouse down, and laid a red-hot poker against her third vertebra. Shaking with pain, Odette still refused to reply. She was told to remove her shoes and stockings. In his biography of Odette (1949), Jerrard Tickell described what followed:

'Odette gazed incredulously ... at the red litter on the floor, litter of diabolical chiropody'

A man knelt at her feet ... He took her left foot in his left hand and settled the steel jaws of the pincers tightly around the tip of her nail. Then with a slow, muscular drag, he began to pull. A semi-circle of blood started to the quick, oozed over the skin, flooded after the retreating nail ... He shook the pincers and her nail fell on the floor ...

The pincers clasped the next nail, gripped hard, were slowly drawn back. The enclosing flesh ripped and yielded in agonizing pain as the nail was dragged out. ... She gave no cry. After an eternity, her torturer stood up ... Odette gazed incredulously at the bloody furnace of her feet and at the red litter on the floor, litter of a diabolical chiropody.

Before her torturer could do the same to her fingernails, a senior Gestapo officer entered the room and ordered him to stop. Several days later Odette was sentenced to death by a military tribunal, but, as the Gestapo still wished to question her, she was kept in Fresnes for over a year. She was later consigned to the women's concentration camp at Ravensbrück. Miraculously, she survived.

Another agent tortured by the Gestapo was Forest Yeo-Thomas. In 1944 he was first taken to Gestapo quarters in the rue de Saussaies. There he was beaten, and then, with his hands manacled behind him and a chain round his ankles, flung into a bath of cold water. Just as he was drowning, he was dragged from the bath and revived – a treatment repeated several times. After this, he was repeatedly beaten again.

The following afternoon, Yeo-Thomas was taken to a small room in 84 Avenue Foch, where his handcuffs were attached to a hook on the end of a long chain hanging from a pulley on the ceiling, and he was raised until his heels were off the ground. According to a description in Bruce Marshall's *The White Rabbit*: 'Agony shot through his shoulders, a red film obscured his eyes and, unable to restrain himself, he groaned ... In intermittent spells of consciousness he suffered pain worse than any he had so far endured. Not until it was dark did they loosen him, and at once he crumpled up on the floor.'

Later, he was chained to a desk with his legs spread, while three men with rubber coshes beat his face, body, and testicles. Then, as far as he could remember, he was half-drowned and artificially revived another six times. When his handcuffs were removed, he saw his hands for the first time since he had been hung from the chain. 'The handcuffs were rusty with blood, the flesh round his badly cut wrists was purple, and his left arm was swollen up to the elbow.'

Captured members of the Resistance suffered as badly, particularly at the hands of the notorious Klaus Barbie in Lyon. André Pédron, who survived the concentration camp at Belsen, described the torture of the bath in Henri Amouroux's *Grande histoire des Français sous l'occupation* (1983):

> You've seen how Arabs carry a sheep, tied by its feet to a pole they carry on their shoulders? Then they immerse you, placing the rod across the bath. It becomes a spit on which they turn you, pulling you by the hair.

In the same book, another captured Resistance fighter, Dubreuil, describes how he had his fingers and genitals crushed in a door. In agony, he let slip some details. The next day a female member of the network, Brigitte Friang, was arrested; she received a bullet wound in the belly, and was flung into a prison cell:

> The sound of footsteps on the flagstones of the passage. That's it, it's for me. It's time for the first great confrontation ... I was so terrified that I

The Gestapo chief Klaus Barbie – who was eventually brought to trial for his crimes in Lyon in 1987 – was responsible for the torture and execution of many people suspected of collaboration with the French Resistance. On one occasion in 1944, he ordered the mass execution of 88 prisoners.

trembled all over. They must not see. I hid my shuddering hands beneath the blanket. A current of sweat – the sweat of fear – poured down my back …

First she was beaten systematically: on the top of her head, her temples, her jaws. Fist blows slammed her head against the wall. Then her torturer – a French collaborator – turned his attention to her wounds. Beaten on the belly, she screamed; though she later wrote that this was more in fury than in pain. He left off her belly, and began to pinch, pull, slap and punch, first at her face, and then at her breasts:

> Slamming punches into a woman's breasts, that must be satisfying. That must appease all sorts of petty resentments … That must make you feel very manly … it must be particularly exciting, when they are the breasts of a 20-year-old.

No suspect was exempt from the tortures of the Gestapo or their French collaborators. The abbé Boursier was 66 years old when he was arrested in June 1944. Before his death – in a mass execution with 87 others, ordered by Klaus Barbie – he was submitted four times to the torture of the bath. Raymond Valeriot was tortured by his fellow-countrymen of the *Brigades Spéciales*: 'When I wouldn't talk, they threatened to crush my testicles between two boards and turn me over to the Gestapo.' Yves Gaillot had his eyes torn out with a fork. It is small wonder that when the tide of war turned and France was liberated, the Resistance took a terrible revenge upon their torturers.

Prisoners of the Japanese

During the war in the Far East, the Allied prisoners of war suffered most. The Japanese warrior code considered surrender to be shameful, and the prisoners had to suffer contemptuous ill-treatment at the hands of their captors. They were driven to forced labour, given the most meagre of rations, frequently beaten with canes or whips, and sometimes prodded with bayonets, whenever they protested.

In *Bamboo and Bushido*, Alfred Allbury described a common scene: 'What might have been mistaken for a number of lifesize, nearly naked, statues dotted about the dock area were in fact recalcitrant PoWs poised on drums and boxes, holding above their heads shovels, spades or picks, and forced to stare open-eyed into the blazing sun.'

But this could be considered a relatively mild punishment, compared with some of those described in Kenneth Harrison's *The Brave Japanese*.

'Slamming punches into a woman's breasts, …That must appease all sorts of petty resentments'

(The title is not ironic; Harrison, who suffered badly at their hands, nevertheless maintained that the Japanese were outstandingly brave soldiers.)

Men were flogged on the triangle, or subjected to mock hangings, being reprieved only at the last moment. Prisoners might be 'given salt water for days, then allowed to drink their fill of cold clear water, after which they were jumped on or punched heavily in the stomach, so that water gushed from their eyes, mouth and nostrils'. Some were hung by their feet, while urine, or sometimes iodine, was poured into their nostrils. Others were made to kneel for hours on sharp stones.

The war in Algeria

In view of the sufferings of Resistance fighters at the hands of the Gestapo in France, it is surprising that the French Army resorted to torture during the war in Algeria (1954–62).

From 1848 until 1962, Algeria was constitutionally a part of 'metropolitan' France, but in fact had the characteristics of a colony. The majority of the population were Moslems, who were dominated by a relatively small number

The invading Japanese treated their Allied prisoners with barbarity during World War II. Here an Australian airman is being publicly executed, 'samurai style'.

of economically and politically powerful European settlers, known as *pieds noirs*. On 1 November 1954, a nationalist revolution broke out, with guerrilla attacks being carried out by the *Front de Libération Nationale* (FLN) on French and *pied noir* targets.

The French Army responded rapidly, destroying the central organization of the FLN, but the attacks continued. In January 1957 General Jacques Massu's 10th Parachute Division entered the city of Algiers, rounded up and interrogated suspects under torture. As a result of information obtained, one of the surviving FLN leaders, Ben M'Hidi, was captured. Nine days later, an Army press officer announced that he had 'committed suicide by hanging himself in his cell …'.

*Smiling French 'paras'
threaten a prisoner
during the Battle
of Algiers, 1957–9.
Torture was widespread,
and more than 3000
prisoners 'disappeared'
after interrogation.*

Soon, conflicting reports about his death began to emerge: it was said that M'Hidi attempted to hang himself with an electric flex, and was 'still breathing' when taken to hospital; two medical officers stated that he was dead before reaching hospital, and 'our attention was not attracted by apparent marks of wounds'. It transpired that he had been handed over to a 'special section' of paras who 'interrogated him on their own initiative, and killed him'.

The growing rumours of torture and summary executions caused public disquiet in France. Torture had been expressly abolished on 8 October 1789, but as Jean-Paul Sartre wrote in 1958: 'Torture is neither civilian nor military … it is a plague infecting our whole era.'

A sinister perspective is given to the matter by the Wuillaume Report, drawn up by a senior civil servant in 1955, which proposed that the use of torture by the police should be legalized in France – *because* it had become so widespread. Although the Wuillaume Report was rejected, it seems that torture by means of electricity and water, and by other means, had been employed by the gendarmes in Algeria for many years.

During the 'Battle of Algiers', Colonel Roger Trinquier was responsible for intelligence-gathering. He already had experience in torturing suspects in Indo-China (subsequently Vietnam), and his methods strikingly recall those of the Gestapo. The city was divided into sectors, subsectors, blocks, and buildings, and a reliable Moslem informer was assigned to each block. This *blockleiter* (the Nazi equivalent) had the duty of reporting all suspicious activities in his block.

It has been estimated that, during the Battle of Algiers, between 30 and 40 per cent of the entire male population of the Casbah were arrested and handed over to a Détachement Opérationnel de Protection (DOP), described by General Massu as 'specialists in the interrogation of suspects who wanted to say nothing'. As Colonel Trinquier wrote: 'If the suspect makes no difficulty about giving the information required, the interrogation will be over quickly; otherwise, specialists must use all means available to drag his secret out of him.'

A priest who was recalled to the colours, and served as an officer in Algeria during 1958 and 1959, wrote:

> we are told during the intelligence course that there is a 'humane' type of torture ... Captain L. gave us five points, which I took down *in extenso*, with all the objections and replies: (1) The torture must be decent; (2) it must not take place in the presence of young people; (3) it must not take place in the presence of sadists; (4) it must be carried out under an officer or responsible authority; (5) it must be humane, i.e. once the man begins to talk, it must stop; and, above all, it must leave no traces. In consideration of which, ran the conclusion, 'you are entitled to water and electricity'.

The electrical torture was known as the *gégène*, from the first syllable of *générateur*. It employed an army signals magneto, with electrodes that could be fastened to any part of the body, particularly the penis.

Henri Alleg, editor of the *Alger Républicain*, and a European Jew whose family had settled in Algeria during World War II, was held under interrogation by the paras for a month in 1957. In his first experience with the *gégène*, the electrodes were attached to one finger and an ear:

> A flash of lightning exploded next to my ear, and I felt my heart racing in my breast. [Then a larger magneto was used.] Instead of the sharp and rapid spasms that seemed to tear my body in two, it was now a greater pain that took possession of all my muscles, and tightened them in longer spasms. [Next the electrodes were placed in his mouth.] My jaws were

'Torture is neither civilian nor military ... it is a plague infecting our whole era.'

Colonel Roger Trinquier, chief of intelligence during the Battle of Algiers. He already had experience of torturing prisoners in French Indo-China (Vietnam), and his methods were strikingly like those of the Gestapo.

soldered to the electrode by the current, and it was impossible for me to unlock my teeth, no matter what effort I made.

The water torture took various forms: victims' bellies and lungs were filled from a hose placed in the mouth, with the nose held closed; or their heads were plunged repeatedly into a trough. Paratrooper Pierre Leulliette described one Alsatian sergeant, whose clients 'were often choking with apprehension long before they touched the water … He would have liked to interrogate Europeans, but they were rare.'

One of the first to protest against the use of torture in Algeria was General Jacques de Bollardière, who arrived in Algeria in late 1956. Bollardière told General Massu that the orders he had been given were 'in absolute opposition to the respect of man, which was the foundation of my life'. He wrote to the army commander-in-chief, requesting a posting back to France. On 27 March 1957 he wrote to the newspaper *L'Express*, drawing attention to 'the terrible danger there would be for us to lose sight … of the moral values that alone have … created the grandeur of our civilization and of our army'. For this breach of discipline, he was sentenced to 60 days of 'fortress arrest'.

Two days later, the secretary-general of the Algiers prefecture, Paul Teitgen (see the Introduction, page 7), handed in his resignation, writing that he had 'recognized on certain detainees profound traces of the cruelties and tortures that I personally suffered 14 years ago in the Gestapo cellars'.

Teitgen was persuaded to keep his letter secret, and to retain his office. He was accorded powers of detention, which meant, theoretically, that the paras could not imprison suspects. The worst excesses were moderated, but in September Teitgen gave up the struggle because torture was still being employed. He calculated that by this time more than 3000 Algerians had 'disappeared'.

How they disappeared was described in a letter from a young soldier:

They used to ask for volunteers to finish off the guys who had been tortured – there are no marks left that way, and so no danger of a witch-hunt later. I didn't like the idea – you know how it is, shooting a chap a hundred metres [328 feet] off in battle, that's nothing, because the guy's some way off, and you can hardly see him. And anyway, he's armed, and can either shoot back or buzz off. But finishing off a defenceless guy just like that … He looked at me. I can see his eyes looking at me now. The whole thing revolted me. I fired. The other chaps finished off the rest. After that it wasn't so bad. But the first time, I tell you that turned me up.

Pierre Leulliette described having 'to bury one of the suspects, who had died at their [the DOP's] hands, in the quicklime at the bottom of the garden'. And there were reports of bodies dropped by helicopter out at sea, and of a mass grave some 30km (19 miles) from Algiers.

The hostilities dragged on. In France, in the spring of 1958, Charles de Gaulle was persuaded to return from political exile, and form a government. In a broadcast on 16 September 1959, he spoke of 'self determination' for Algeria. Both the *pieds noirs* and the paras felt themselves betrayed, and with the cry of *Algerie française!*, they created their own terrorist group, the *Organisation Armée Secrète* (OAS). However, French public opinion was behind de Gaulle, and Algeria finally achieved independence in March 1962.

But the legacy of torture survived, in its effect both upon those who had suffered it, and those who had practised it. A police inspector in France, later found guilty of torturing his own wife and children, explained that he had been deeply influenced by what he had been required to do to Algerian prisoners: 'The thing that kills me most is the torture. You just don't know what it's like, do you?'

And as Louis Joxe, who negotiated the final peace settlement, said: 'I shall never forget the young officers and soldiers whom I met, who were absolutely appalled by what they had to do.'

Torture worldwide

It is ironic that those countries that were among the first to throw off the Spanish and Portuguese colonial yoke – and with it the terror of the Inquisition – have, during the twentieth century, themselves become notorious for the ill-treatment of both criminal and political prisoners. Amnesty International (see Chapter 13, page 186) has highlighted cases in nearly every one of the Latin American countries. Many of these have also involved young and innocent children.

In Argentina, Bolivia, Chile and Mexico, the organization has reported frequent beatings, 'directed specifically at the genitals' and threats – or actual cases – of sexual assault. Under the military *junta* that ruled Argentina between 1976 and 1983, 'abduction and torture, frequently followed by murder, of political opponents became a systematic practice of the regime'.

Many victims were never seen again, and became known as *desaparecidos*, the 'disappeared'. A 'National Commission on the Disappeared', set up by the new Argentine government in 1984, reported that at least 9000 persons had suffered this fate, many after enduring long periods of torture in secret detention centres. Independent organizations,

'He would have liked to interrogate Europeans, but they were rare'

such as the local *Madres de Plaza*, estimated that the figure could be nearer 30,000.

A small group of forensic experts has set up a team to investigate the cause and manner of death of skeletal remains recovered from mass burials. They have been assisted by forensic anthropologists from other countries, such as the famous American, Clyde Snow. The evidence uncovered includes patterned rib fractures, amputations of fingers, fractures of limbs, and traumatic injuries to teeth.

Brutal treatment of prisoners by the police occurs in many Latin American countries. In Bolivia, *la campaña* ('the bell') leaves no physical sign of injury. The victim's head is placed inside a metal container, which is then beaten repeatedly: the noise and the vibration are unbearable. Police in Chile and Mexico favour *el teléfono* (the telephone), which involves incessant blows to the ears. In Ecuador, Reinero Jurado described his interrogation by soldiers in 1993: 'I had a water bag put over my head, then they sprayed me.'

Mexican police also employ a torture known as *la chicharra* ('the buzzer'). An electric prod is attached to the eyes, gums, tongue, nipples and genitals. Parts of the victim's body may also be forced into light fittings, or attached to the mains by cables.

But it is not only in Latin America that torture is still employed. Although it was virtually discontinued in Algeria for some years, it is now common practice again. A favoured method is *le chiffon*, very similar to the technique described by Eremundus Frisius (see Chapter 4, pages 62–63). The victim is tied to a bench or suspended from a bar, a piece of cloth is packed into his mouth, and dirty water is poured on it. In 1994, Noureddine Lamdjadani suffered this treatment over a period of 57 days.

The secret police in Chad employ the *supplice de baguettes*. A cord is tied round the victim's head, and then twisted with two sticks. This causes intense pain, and, in due course, haemorrhages from the nose, and loss of consciousness. In Syria, detainees suffer *al-kursi al-Almani*, the 'German chair'. They are strapped into a metal frame with a movable backrest: this is then lowered, resulting in extension

Possibly the youngest innocent victim to be tortured by the secret police in Chile. Three-year-old Tamara was denied food and beaten, and had her head immersed in ice-cold water, over a period of four days. She and her family eventually escaped to Sweden.

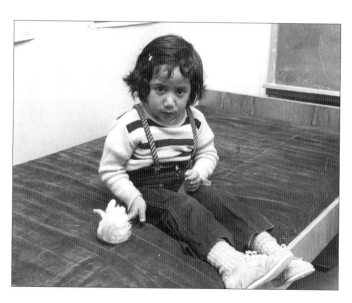

of the spine, and acute pressure on the neck and limbs. This can lead to asphyxiation, loss of consciousness, and fracture of the verterbrae.

In China, many of the tortures practised under the old Manchu dynasty (see Chapter 9) are still in use. One guard at a detention centre in Shaanxi Province boasted that he knew 39 ways of shackling a prisoner. A particularly painful form is known as 'Su Qin carries a sword on his back'. One of the prisoner's arms is pulled over his shoulder, and shackled to the other, which is twisted up behind his back. Other punishments are called 'bending three wheels', or 'the old ox ploughing the land'. Even more brutal tortures include *dian ji* (electric assault), *jiaxin mian bao* (the sandwich filling), and *zuo feiji* (the jetplane ride).

In Myanmar (Burma) victims are taken for a 'helicopter ride'. They are hung by their wrists or ankles from a rotating ceiling fan, and beaten as it turns. In India, the 'aeroplane' is a simpler device: the detainee is beaten while his arms are bound to a pole resting on his shoulders. And in Sudan, when 'the plane takes off', the prisoner's elbows are tied to his knees, and a wooden pole is pushed through the gap. 'He is left hanging for days. They give him drops of water and keep flogging him.'

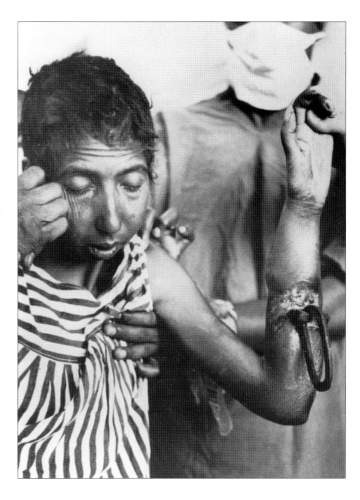

This Yemeni woman fled from her cruel husband, but was recaptured. The iron ring was nailed into her arm by order of the Yemen court.

There are many more countries, reported by Amnesty International, in which torture still occurs, including Sri Lanka, Pakistan, Afghanistan, Iraq, Indonesia, the Philippines, El Salvador and Haiti. Israel has been openly accused of torture. The methods of the Turkish police are infamous, and the Greek police have a deserved reputation for brutality. In Bulgaria and Romania, members of racial minorities have been subjected to vicious beatings. And full details of the crimes committed during the 'ethnic cleansing' of Bosnia are only now beginning to emerge.

Chapter Twelve
Torture of the Mind

The use of psychological rather than physical pressure in interrogation and the obtaining of confessions has been employed for centuries, but was brought to a high level of sophistication in the twentieth century. It can conveniently be divided into two types, although the actual effects are generally the outcome of a combination of both.

The first instrument of psychological torture is fear: the preliminary stage of an enquiry generally has been the showing of the instruments of torment, or at least the threat that physical methods will be used. In hundreds of historical cases, this has proved to be sufficient to obtain a confession.

In more recent times, the staging of mock executions has been employed. On the morning of 22 December 1849, the Russian writer Fyodor Dostoyevsky, with some 20 others found guilty of sedition, was marched on to the Semenovski parade ground in Moscow. The sentence of death was read out with agonizing slowness by a general who was famous for his stutter. Just as the firing squad was being given its orders, an aide galloped up with a sealed paper from Tsar Nicholas I. Laboriously, the general opened it and announced its contents: the sentences had been commuted to imprisonment in Siberia. It turned out that the entire charade had been planned by the Tsar.

Similar techniques have been used, with varying degrees of sophistication, in more recent times. This was sometimes done out of what appears to be sheer sadism, rather than to obtain information. Nazi troops in Italy (and more than likely personnel on both sides in other theatres of war) are known to have forced captive Allied soldiers to dig their own graves whilst being subjected to graphic descriptions of what was about to happen to them. The latter were unnecessary unless this were a mock execution intended to extract information. It was not; the captives were simply executed without being interrogated.

Elaborate mock executions have been used at other times to break down the subject's will to resist. In many modern cases of mock execution by firing squad, victims have heard the shots and only gradually realized that they are still alive. The exhaustion and mix of intense emotions

(Opposite) American pilots, prisoners of the North Vietnamese during the Vietnam War, 1965–71. Many prisoners were subjected to 'brainwashing' techniques, which had begun in China as a tool of the political indoctrination programme.

caused by the experience can break even a strong will, and the shock may well be sufficient to produce lifelong intellectual damage.

Other ways to induce fear, or to use it, include leaving the subject alone for a while. Someone who is confined and entirely in the power of their captors, and who has reason to expect that they will be tortured, is likely to torment themselves with imaginary versions of what might happen. Every footfall outside the door can induce stark terror; a guard walking past or even bringing food can raise fear to a new pitch.

This approach requires that the subject have a reason to fear torture or death, and thus must be set up by the captors. As already noted, showing the subject the instruments of torture can work, or actually torturing him and then leaving him to reflect upon his experiences. Other methods include the relatively subtle gambit of allowing him to see fellow captives removed from the holding area never to return, or forcing the subject to witness torture or executions, or making him clean up the mess and bury the bodies.

The key to using fear as a means of torture is to induce the subject to torture himself. He must have a strong reason to fear, and must not become inured to it. Eventually the fear of physical torture diminishes either because it does not happen or, ironically perhaps, because it does. Incredible as it may seem, being tortured can become somehow normal unless a variety of methods are used. It is also generally more effective for physical as well as psychological reasons to hurt a subject then let him rest and reflect on the experience rather than continuing the session.

Hooding the subject deprives him of some sensory input and encourages reflection on his fears of what might come next. Small and fairly innocuous sounds can become terrifying as the subject imagines what they might signify.

For maximum effectiveness of fear as an instrument of torture, it is important that the subject has something to lose. A victim who is resigned to pain and eventual death may resist torture and not give up information as a way of wringing a sort of victory out of the situation. However, someone who has something to lose can be influenced more greatly. This could mean threats to arrest and torture the subject's friends and family if he does not cooperate, in effect giving him a positive reason to talk (to protect his loved ones) rather than a purely negative one (to end the suffering).

A more subtle version of this gambit is to give the subject something that can later be taken away. There are tales of British soldiers confined to the glasshouse – notorious hard cases subject to a fairly mild form of confinement – reduced to tears by being told that two of the six boiled sweets that were their only privilege that day were being withheld for minor infractions. Taking everything away from someone can make them stronger. Taking away nearly everything can make what little remains so precious that the fear of losing it becomes unbearable.

The other instrument of psychological torture is disorientation. This can be produced in various ways. The conditions of imprisonment itself, in a damp, cold (or sometimes deliberately overheated) cell, frequently without daylight, make it extremely difficult to keep track of the passing of time. If food and drink are withheld, or brought at irregular intervals, prisoners become further confused and, in due course, may lose all confidence in their own personalities.

Sleep deprivation was advocated by Hippolytus de Marsiliis in the sixteenth century (see Chapter 3, page 44), and employed by Matthew Hopkins to obtain confessions from East Anglian witches 100 years later (see Chapter 7, page 117). In Soviet Russia – at the time of Stalin's purge of all his old comrades during the 1930s – it was refined into what became known as the 'conveyor' system, in which relays of examiners could keep prisoners under interrogation for days at a time. Sergei Bessonov, who was one of the prosecution witnesses in the trial of Nicolai Krestinsky, was nevertheless himself subjected to this treatment, being interrogated continuously for 17 days without food or sleep.

Similar methods have been employed, unofficially, by modern European and American police – a process known colloquially as the 'third degree'. (Interestingly, this name is derived from the ceremony of entry to the Third Degree of Freemasonry, that of Master Mason, in which the candidate is subjected to a lengthy interrogation, and undergoes a symbolic ritual of death.)

Incredible as it may seem, being tortured can become somehow normal unless a variety of methods are used.

there is firm evidence that psychological torture has been used in the interrogation of IRA suspects

In America during the 1930s, third degree interrogation by the police took a variety of forms. Sometimes the prisoner was physically assaulted (a process known to the French police as passage à tabac – a phrase best translated as 'running the gauntlet'), but most often the treatment was basically psychological. The prisoner was seated in a darkened room, with a brilliant desk light shining directly into his face. The interrogating detective sat, almost invisible, behind the lamp; in answering his questions, the prisoner found himself gazing straight into the dazzling light. At the same time, he was conscious of other detectives – silent but accusing – in the room behind him.

A cunning development of this method of interrogation was the concept of the Bad and Good Detectives. After a harrowing questioning by one man, who shouted, thumped his desk, and offered violence, the prisoner would be left alone for a short while, before being joined by another man, who turned the light away from his eyes, and provided refreshment and a cigarette.

'Listen,' this man would say, 'I don't approve of the way you've been treated. It's not right. Why don't you tell me what it's all about? If you confide in me, I'll see that you don't have to go through all that again.'

A variation on this approach was the use of a 'stool pigeon'. Another prisoner, suborned by the police – or somebody who was apparently a prisoner – would be put into the same holding cell, and would encourage the first prisoner to talk about the crime for which he or she had been arrested.

Although these methods have been condemned, and the use of the third degree has largely fallen into disuse, there is no doubt that they are still practised by many police forces. American law still relies on confessions given 'voluntarily' or of 'free will'. However, in England and Wales the admissibility of such 'voluntary' confessions has been restricted by the Police and Criminal Evidence Act of 1984. Confessions are excluded from evidence if it is judged that they have been obtained by methods or in conditions that are likely to render them 'unreliable'. They can also be excluded if they are found to have been obtained by 'oppression' of the person confessing.

The law is different in Scotland and Northern Ireland. In Northern Ireland, there is firm evidence that psychological torture has been used in the interrogation of IRA suspects. Amnesty International reported that 'confessions' were obtained by deprivation of sleep, food, and drink, enforced prolonged standing, hooding, the use of continuous noise, and other methods of 'depth interrogation'. Such methods were employed by the police and by members of the British Army.

Disorientation techniques continued in the Soviet Union long after the interrogation of political prisoners during the 1930s. Lavrenti Beria became Minister of the Interior, and head of the police, in 1938. On Stalin's death in 1953 he attempted to seize power, but was shot after a secret trial. This 1953 photograph shows how prisoners were interrogated during his reign of terror.

Drugs and brainwashing

Many modern writers have suggested that since the original legal justification for torture was the necessity to obtain information, all forms of physical suffering could be replaced successfully, without pain, by the use of drugs. However, the administration of any drug, without the consent of the person receiving it, is an invasion of the personality, and – even more importantly – is a practice too easily subject to abuse.

Much has been made in recent years of the so-called 'truth drugs'. The most common of these is thiopental, often popularly known as sodium pentothal. This is a barbiturate with a very short term of action, sometimes used as a general anaesthetic for dental operations. It has been suggested that in a relaxed state close to unconsciousness – either immediately after administration of the drug, or on the gradual return to consciousness – people can be persuaded to tell the truth that they have previously concealed. Claims for the success of this technique have been disputed. In any case, evidence obtained in this way would not be acceptable in most courts of law.

Guerrilla warfare for independence in Rhodesia (now Zimbabwe) lasted from 1977 to 1980. These prisoners were forced to maintain this position in the heat of the midday sun, while a Rhodesian trooper repeatedly clicked the trigger of his gun in their faces.

Conversely, the method has sometimes proved successful with people who have themselves requested the use of thiopental in order to establish that they have been telling the truth all along.

There is no doubt that drugs have been employed in interrogations, and as a means of torture. In Uruguay during the 1970s doctors assisted in the administration of a variety of drugs that produced hallucinations, or sensations of acute pain and asphyxiation. It was reported that those doctors who resisted the demands of the torturers were 'disappeared' – so many of them, that the healthcare programme of the country reached a state of crisis.

The barbiturate drugs, such as thiopental, come within a large group known as hypnotics. This name means 'sleep-inducing' – but it raises the idea that hypnosis might be used as a means of interrogation. There is no firm evidence that this method has been tried, but, in any case, it is well established that people under hypnosis cannot be made to perform acts unwillingly. However, as a subtle means of torture it might prove attractive to the sadist: there is strong evidence that inexperienced or careless hypnotists can cause lasting psychological damage to their subjects.

Related to these other psychological techniques is the process of 'thought reform' known colloquially as 'brainwashing'. It has been employed in various forms for centuries, by the Inquisition, and in both Tsarist and Soviet Russia, but it is particularly associated with the methods of the Chinese Communists in the twentieth century, to whom it is known as hsi nao.

Brainwashing began as a tool of the Chinese political indoctrination programme, which was based on the concept that those who have not been educated in communist dogma have wrong 'bourgeois' attitudes, and must be 're-educated'. It was applied to all those who were considered politically unreliable – not only intellectuals but peasants and soldiers – and also to European and American prisoners during the Korean and Vietnam wars.

The technique is devoted to the destruction of a person's self-image by physical pressures, humiliation, and the production of a feeling of guilt; this self-image is then reconstructed in intensive study in closely knit groups.

Prisoners are denied their normal daily routines, and have to submit to a regime that requires unquestioning obedience – eating, sleeping, and performing their natural functions, according to a strict schedule, doing nothing without the permission of their guards, and keeping heads bowed in their presence. Any refusal to cooperate is punished by deprivation of food and sleep, or by chaining.

Any easing of this harsh regime must be won by redemption. Prison officials and fellow cell-mates (many of them who already well on the way to conversion) exert continual pressure on the prisoners to make them reconsider their pasts in the light of communist belief, recognize their guilt, and, eventually, confess their crimes. Long interrogations and 'struggle meetings' employ all available means to keep up the pressure, and daily study groups are devoted to the learning of communist doctrine.

Once the prisoners have confessed their guilt, and demonstrated that they have been satisfactorily re-educated, they are brought to trial and convicted, but are then given a lenient sentence in recognition of their reform.

The entire process may take up to four years to complete. Whether the psychological change is permanent or not seems to depend upon the individual's strength of character and subsequent environment. The use of brainwashing, coupled with hypnosis, is the basis of the plot of Richard Condon's novel, and the subsequent film, *The Manchurian Candidate* (1960), in which an American prisoner is programmed to attempt the assassination of the US president. Fortunately this was only fiction.

The technique is devoted to the destruction of a person's self-image by physical pressures

Chapter Thirteen

Torture Post 9/11

Attacks on the World Trade Centre and other targets on September 11th, 2001 demonstrated that terrorists can strike anywhere. The key to combating them is information, but if captured terrorists and their supporters are treated with extreme gentleness they have no real incentive to give up information. It is simply not realistic to declare that any form of harshness is morally unacceptable and refrain from doing it.

The question is what degree of harshness is acceptable in our troubled modern world? Where is the compromise between methods that give a realistic chance of obtaining information that will save lives, and outright torture? Does it make a difference if the subject is known for certain to be a 'bad guy'? Is it relevant to consider whether information eventually extracted by non-torture methods would be too late to be useful? A line has to be drawn somewhere between what is unpleasant but acceptable and what is not, and in a situation where innocents are under attack the luxury of taking a distant moral viewpoint may not be affordable.

One way to avoid having to answer this question is to hand off captives to someone else and use the information they send back without question. There have been allegations that the British government has done exactly this in recent years, passing captives to those who it knows will torture them in return for any information obtained.

In addition to being morally questionable, this approach runs the risk of creating believable false information. If no questions are asked about how a given piece of intelligence was obtained, it is difficult to ascertain whether or not it is reliable. Placing faith in such information can result, at best, in difficult questions being asked later and might lead to serious mistakes when the intelligence is acted upon.

Iraq

Operation Iraqi Freedom, launched in 2003 with the intention of toppling the brutal regime of Saddam Hussein in Iraq, remains controversial to this day. The war itself was quickly won and Saddam Hussein was removed from power. However, attempts to set up a moderate and sustainable government in Iraq were hampered by an ongoing insurgency.

(Opposite)
Waterboarding is one of several forms of 'water torture' designed to make the subject suffer the sensation of drowning. It is sometimes considered to be not-quite-torture and therefore acceptable, though it is hard to see the justification for this viewpoint.

Fear of death was also not much of a factor for many. Yet information had to be extracted

Combating this threat was a complex business, in which information and intelligence played a critical role. Information from captured insurgents or their supporters could prevent more Western soldiers or innocent Iraqi civilians being killed. In this light, it is not hard to see how harsh interrogations seemed necessary. Many of the insurgents were fanatical in their hatred of the West and thus more or less immune to inducements to make a deal. Fear of death was also not much of a factor for many. Yet information had to be extracted.

Before the war began, the US government considered the legality of what are known as enhanced interrogation techniques. These included the use of stress positions, in which the subject is forced to remain in a position that causes severe muscle strain for an extended period, sleep deprivation and waterboarding. The latter requires that the subject be restrained on an inclined board with his feet slightly higher than his head. The face is covered with a cloth onto which water is poured. In addition to a drowning sensation, the subject is likely to have vomit travelling up his oesophagus, which can result in death if it enters the lungs.

Waterboarding is a horrific psychological experience which is often, but not always, considered to be torture. The common justification for waterboarding is that it does not directly cause physical harm, though severe physical effects are possible as the subject struggles against restraints. Along with other methods, waterboarding was considered as a possible measure in the interrogation of certain high-value captives.

Although it was a widely-stated position of the US government in the months just after Operation Iraqi Freedom that waterboarding did not constitute torture, this position was later revised and the practice was banned. Analysis of intelligence gathered in Iraq and the results of action taken based upon it suggest that little – if any – information that could be used to save lives was obtained by these methods. This agrees with conventional wisdom regarding the use of torture. A subject is likely to give false information to bring the torture to an end, which may be useful if the object is to extract a false confession for propaganda purposes but is far less valuable if actionable intelligence is desired.

Most of the useful information gained in the Iraq conflict was obtained by methods ranging from lengthy conventional interrogation to simple bribery. Another factor was the polite, respectful and restrained behaviour of Western personnel towards the civilian population of Iraq, which won over many people to the point where they offered information voluntarily. The actions of those who did not follow this policy were counterproductive, damaging relations between Western troops and the Iraqi population. The worst excesses were at the Abu Ghraib prison.

Abu Ghraib

Abu Ghraib prison, located close to Baghdad, was used by the Coalition as both a forward operating base and detention centre after the fall of the Saddam Hussein regime. It gained notoriety in the West due to scandals over the mistreatment of prisoners there, but was well known as a place of torture and suffering long before 2003. Mass graves nearby hold the bodies of many prisoners executed at Abu Ghraib, and torture was commonplace there.

After the fall of Saddam Hussein, Abu Ghraib was an obvious choice to hold both criminals and captured insurgents. The prison was of course a grim place with a bad reputation, but those guarding the prisoners were expected to behave humanely. However, in 2003 reports of human rights abuses at Abu Ghraib began to emerge. Some of the allegations concerned what might be considered routine mistreatment such as failing to provide protection from heat and cold, or food, or striking prisoners for very minor infractions. How prevalent such mistreatment was remains unclear, as does the degree to which it was necessary to strike or punish inmates. Abu Ghraib housed many determined insurgents

This image from Abu Ghraib prison has become notorious worldwide, fostering the belief that the torture of detainees was prevalent there. It may never be possible to determine the true extent of abuse at the prison, which is now closed.

The detention facility at Guantanamo Bay in Cuba has been at the centre of controversy for some time. Allegations of abuse are rife, but hard evidence is difficult to come by as a result of the extreme security surrounding the installation.

and was subject to several attacks meant to free them. It is obvious that keeping such prisoners under control was difficult, and that guards were right to fear what would happen if they were too lax. Under such conditions the line between harsh control and cruelty becomes blurry. It has been stated that the prison was understaffed and that training for such a difficult situation was lacking. If so, it is possible to see how the line could be crossed without any deliberate intention.

However, evidence emerged of acts that went far beyond this point, and could only have been deliberate. Some, it was alleged, were officially sanctioned as interrogation techniques. These included sleep deprivation, exposure to extremely loud noise and the use of stress positions. Given the US position that certain acts did not – quite – constitute torture and that the Geneva Convention did not apply to military interrogators operating overseas, this seems likely to be true. If so, the use of torture might be justified by those who carried it out or authorised it as a necessary part of the war against the Iraqi insurgents. There is, however, no way to explain some of the acts carried out as anything but cruelty for the sake of it.

Evidence for torture at Abu Ghraib comes from numerous sources, not all of which are reliable. There is clear evidence of both psychological and physical torture of inmates which had nothing to do with interrogation. Many of the methods used were similar to those experienced by US personnel who had undergone training to resist interrogation using torture. This does not necessarily mean that these methods were sanctioned, but those carrying out the torture would use what they knew for the most part. A degree of sadistic invention was also present.

Prisoners were subjected to a variety of measures which were designed to break down pride and ego in order to make an interrogation subject more malleable, but in this case were probably just used for the sake of harming the victim. Much of the abuse was sexual, either directly as rape and sodomy or by forcing prisoners to perform sex acts. Nakedness was used to add to the humiliation of other acts, which ranged from beatings or being dragged around the floor to forcing prisoners into a sort of human pyramid. There are allegations that guards made prisoners crawl around on all fours whilst riding on their backs, and that prisoners were executed or died as a result of punishment for very minor offences.

The strongest evidence for abuse at Abu Ghraib came from photographs taken by the guards themselves, often of their comrades apparently enjoying humiliating prisoners. These images caused an outcry in the Western world, though it is notable that in Iraq the reaction was more muted. It seems that the worst excesses revealed in Abu Ghraib post-2003 were relatively mild compared with what had happened there under the Saddam Hussein regime.

Be that as it may, the situation was complex and was further confused by various attempts to defend at least some of the actions taken there, or by some officials to distance themselves from the controversy. It may never be clear exactly what went on in Abu Ghraib prison nor who was guilty of what, but the US did remove a number of personnel from duty, punished some within the service and imprisoned others. Abu Ghraib prison was returned to the Iraqi government and eventually closed in 2014, but controversy over the events there continues.

Guantanamo Bay Detention Camp

Guantanamo Bay Detention Camp was established in 2002 with the intention of providing high security for highly dangerous prisoners. Its location outside the USA offered a legal loophole, apparently granting exemption from the Geneva Convention and various aspects of judicial process. This position was challenged and overturned by a series of legal decisions starting 2004, in which the US Supreme Court ruled that the courts did have jurisdiction and that evidence suspected of being obtained by coercion was inadmissible.

Many of those held at Guantanamo Bay had a vague legal status. Often there was insufficient evidence to charge them with any crime or to treat them as captured insurgents, but they were considered too dangerous to simply release. Detention without trial was the only option, but this is not acceptable to a large segment of the Western public. There have been many allegations that during this period of detention coercive interrogation has been used. Many of those detained at Guantanamo were not high-value personnel; others were suspects against whom the evidence was scanty. Guantanamo thus served as a sort of limbo into which captives could be placed until there was a better idea of what to do with them – which might be never. Thus many of those detained found themselves held in harsh conditions with no prospect for release, and this may account for some of the suicides at the facility.

Among the alleged abuses at Guantanamo Bay are beatings, sleep deprivation, coercive interrogation and religious abuse. The latter is a form of psychological torture in which detainees are forced to endure

There is clear evidence of both psychological and physical torture of inmates which had nothing to do with interrogation

insults to their religion and to witness the destruction of holy books. To those with deeply held beliefs this can be a worse form of humiliation than the same treatment of a person. Sexual abuse, threats to kill or injure detainees with guns or power tools, and humiliation by female interrogators have all been reported as taking place within Guantanamo Bay, as well as more mainstream interrogation techniques such as stress positions and chilling the subject.

Hard proof of any action is difficult to obtain from a high-security facility, and the allegations made by many of those released from the facility are open to question. Despite the difficulty of obtaining hard evidence of abuses, there are enough allegations and plausible accounts to suggest that torture did take place at the Guantanamo Bay facility. Of course, this is the same thinking that was applied to many detainees – there is a strong suggestion of guilt, but no clear evidence of any specific crime. Whether used to imprison a person or outright condemn the facility detaining them, this assumption of guilt can be dangerous.

The purpose of torture is at least in part to break the will of others by fear

What is known for certain is that Guantanamo Bay is a high security facility in which those suspected of being extremely dangerous enemies are held. Harsh interrogation methods are used there to obtain information or elicit admissions of guilt, and this is an environment in which abuses can easily occur. It is in this sort of environment that the fine line between justifiable harshness and outright cruelty must be most carefully trodden. The detainee population at Guantanamo has been dramatically reduced and that there is a move towards closing it entirely.

ISIS and the Future

ISIS, the so-called Islamic State, which controls parts of Syria and Iraq, openly uses torture and posts videos of its atrocities online. Perhaps the most graphic are public beheadings, but many other forms of torture are used. The intent is rarely to obtain information; to ISIS, torture is about causing fear and thus imposing control over people. Many of the tortures used by ISIS are versions of traditional methods, often distinctive variants previously used by the Saddam Hussein regime in Iraq and the Assad regime in Syria. These include a version of what is sometimes known as the strappado, called *shabe* (ghost) by ISIS. This involves handcuffing the subject's hands behind his back and hoisting him up by them so that his own weight damages his shoulders.

The flying carpet and German chair use a hinged board and an adjustable chair respectively, in both cases the device is adjusted to force the victim's spine into an unnatural alignment, causing intense pain and ultimately damage. Beatings are also routinely used.

This public and open use of torture runs contrary to the beliefs of most nations, who consider it shameful or an unpleasant necessity. But, to groups like ISIS it makes perfect sense to advertise they use torture. The purpose of torture is at least in part to break the will of others by fear. The availability of mass media allows those who openly engage in torture to reach a huge audience and thus to apply what amounts to psychological torture to an audience worldwide. This phenomenon has always existed, but where previously it relied on rumours and second-hand accounts, torture is now centre-stage for anyone to use it openly.

This is ultimately where crossing the line between necessary harshness and deliberate cruelty can lead; beating and beheading someone in front of cameras for the world to see. It is possible to reach the point where this seems desirable by way of a series of small steps. The wholehearted acceptance of torture may be unthinkable today, but the next small step might not. This is what those who adamantly oppose torture fear, and it is what those who have to tread the line must work hard to avoid. The temptation to take that next small step can become overwhelming and once taken there is rarely any going back.

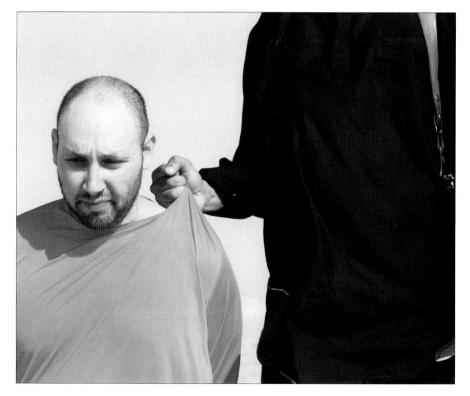

ISIS advertises the fact that it uses torture and murder in order to frighten its enemies and inspire potential followers. There is no moral grey area here; ISIS sees torture as a tool and feels its use to be entirely justified.

Index

Picture Credits

AKG: 14 (Erich Lessing), 17 (Erich Lessing), 30, 38, 40 (Museo del Prado), 45, 49, 63, 64, 65, 78 (Museo del Prado), 93b, 107, 116, 124, 146, 148, 150, 162 (Henning Bock)

Alamy: 189

Alexandra Milgram: 10

Amnesty International: 2

Associated Press: 180

Bridgeman Art Library/ British Library: 35, 36

Camera Press: 8, 167, 170, 172, 173, 174

Corbis: 16 (Library of Congress), 186 (Reuters)

Depositphotos: 176 (Marsan)

Fortean Picture Library: 42, 120, 137

Fotomas Index: 50, 75, 81, 84, 93t, 94, 110, 115, 119, 126

Frank Spooner Pictures: 168

Getty Images: 58, 108, 135, 159

Getty Images/Popperfoto: 160, 165, 179

Hutchison Library: 29 (Juliet Highet)

Mary Evans Picture Library: 33, 46, 52, 60, 68, 100, 129, 132, 152, 156

Peter Newark's Pictures: 6, 12, 18, 20, 22, 24, 25, 26, 28, 55, 57, 66, 70, 72, 76, 82, 86, 89, 90, 92, 97, 98, 103, 104, 109, 113, 118, 122, 139, 140, 142, 154

Photoshot: 185

Royal Armouries: 130 (HM Tower of London, Crown Copyright Reserved)

U.S. Army: 182